A Bible Study by

Melissa Spoelstra

Elijah

Spiritual Stamina in Every Season

Abingdon Women

Nashville

Elijah
Spiritual Stamina in Every Season
Participant Workbook

ISBN 978-1-5018-3891-0

18 19 20 21 22 23 24 25 26 27 — 10 9 8 7 6 5 4 3 2
MANUFACTURED IN THE UNITED STATES OF AMERICA

Contents

About the Author

Melissa Spoelstra is a popular women's conference speaker (including the Aspire Women's Events), Bible teacher, and author who is madly in love with Jesus and passionate about studying God's Word and helping women of all ages to seek Christ and know Him more intimately through serious Bible study. Having a degree in Bible theology, she enjoys teaching God's Word to the body of Christ, traveling to diverse groups and churches across the nation and also to Nairobi, Kenya, for a women's prayer conference. Melissa is the author of the Bible studies *Numbers: Learning Contentment in a Culture of More*; *First Corinthians: Living Love When We Disagree*; *Joseph: The Journey to Forgiveness*; and *Jeremiah: Daring to Hope in an Unstable World*; and the parenting books *Total Family Makeover: 8 Practical Steps to Making Disciples at Home* and *Total Christmas Makeover: 31 Devotions to Celebrate with Purpose*. She has published articles in *ParentLife*, *Women's Spectrum*, *Just Between Us*, and the Women of Faith and Girlfriends in God blogs, and she writes her own regular blog in which she shares her musings about what God is teaching her on any given day. Melissa lives in Dublin, Ohio, with her pastor husband, Sean, and their four kids: Zach, Abby, Sara, and Rachel.

Follow Melissa:

 @MelSpoelstra

 @Daring2Hope

 @Author MelissaSpoelstra

Her blog   MelissaSpoelstra.com
(check here also for event dates and booking information)

Introduction to This Study

Life has its ups and downs. One day it seems that everything is good—with relationships, finances, and emotions all as they should be—and the next it can feel like everything is falling apart. I mentioned to a girlfriend how quickly my emotions can change from one day to the next, and she retorted that hers can change between interstate exits on her drive to work! Sometimes these ups and downs are less momentary and more like seasons. In one season we're at a high point, feeling God's nearness, and in another we're at a low, full of confusion and questions for the Lord. Many times we spend a season between these two extremes, coasting along without much thought to the highs or lows of life. We need spiritual stamina to go the distance with God in *every* season.

The prophet Elijah was no different. He experienced highs and lows too. One moment he was hiding out in the wilderness during a drought, being fed by the ravens, and the next he was on the mountaintop where God showed up in a powerful way with fire and then rain. I can relate to Elijah as he navigated these extremes. He was bold and confident when he heard a word from the Lord and prophesied no rain would fall in the land of Israel, but he was surprised and disappointed when the drought he had predicted affected *his* life along with everyone else's. When the brook dried up, eliminating his water source, he struggled to make sense of God's promises and his very real problems. Have you ever been there?

Like us, Elijah had plenty of ups and downs in his walk with God. From the mountaintop where he called down fire, proving to the world that the Lord is God and exposing counterfeits, to the road where he outran a chariot, demonstrating supernatural strength, Elijah had times when God's power was alive and real to him. Other times, Elijah questioned God and grew weary of life. After the Lord showed up on the mountain, Elijah woke the next morning to learn that an evil queen had placed a price on his head. Elijah told God that he had had enough, even asking God to take his life (1 Kings 19:4). It seems he was worn out with the cycle of mountaintop seasons turning to hiding out seasons, likely with some blah times in between. Perhaps Elijah wasn't wanting death as much as an escape from life as he saw it in that moment: one problem to be solved followed by an even worse predicament. Have you ever felt that way? When the difficulties of living on a planet affected by the curse of sin hit home, have you ever wanted to say "I have had enough," just as Elijah did? I know I have.

Thankfully, there's more to Elijah's story. He expressed his questions, but he persevered as he learned to live by his faith in God rather than his feelings. He developed spiritual stamina, which is the ability to stay true to one's faith and calling through all the ups and downs of life. Because of this spiritual stamina, Elijah was an ordinary person who was able to do extraordinary things for God. He not only finished the race; he finished it well.

We connect with Elijah on so many levels. Like him, we have seen God show up in real ways. God has encouraged us, comforted us, provided for us, and shown Himself real to us through His Word, His presence, and His activity in our lives. Other times the brook has seemed to dry up, and we've been unable to make sense of another challenge, disappointment, or frustration. Through all the highs and lows—and especially those times when we want to quit—we need to stay true to our faith and calling if we want to live fully and finish well. We need spiritual stamina to not only endure but thrive as we carry out the unique mission God has for each of us.

In this study, we will examine the ministry of Elijah, who came to be considered "the great prophet, the man who stands as the pattern for other prophets."[1] Over the next six weeks we'll learn some of the spiritual stamina secrets that helped him hold on and persevere in faith, including practical habits related to the following areas:

1. prayer
2. choices
3. soul care
4. surrender
5. mentoring
6. legacy

Together we'll see that finishing well was Elijah's greatest legacy, and we'll explore how to make that our legacy too. Starting is easy, but finishing well requires stamina!

Whether we happen to be in a mountaintop season where we are experiencing God's power and blessing, a valley season where we feel like running away, or somewhere in between, Elijah's life will inspire us to go the distance in the life of faith. His story will challenge us but not shame us, because we'll discover that he was just as human as we are. Elijah doubted and struggled, but ultimately he chose to believe God. As we study his life—delving into the end of 1 Kings and the beginning of 2 Kings, as well as other references to Elijah's life and ministry in the Old and New Testaments—we will develop perseverance and learn how to hold onto faith regardless of our feelings or circumstances. My prayer is that we will dare to believe God can use us in extraordinary ways as we grow in spiritual stamina in every season!

Options for Study

Before beginning the study, I invite you to consider the level of commitment your time and life circumstances will allow. I have found that what I put into a Bible study directly correlates to what I get out of it. When I commit to do the homework daily, God's truths sink deeper as I take time to reflect and meditate on what God is teaching me. When I am intentional about gathering with other women to watch videos and have discussion, I find that this helps keep me from falling off the Bible study wagon midway. Also, making a point to memorize verses and dig deeper by looking at additional materials greatly benefits my soul.

At other times, however, I have bitten off more than I can chew. When our faith is new, our children are small, or there are great demands on our time because of difficult circumstances or challenges, we need to be realistic about what we will be able to finish. So this study is designed with options that enable you to tailor it for your particular circumstances and needs.

1. Basic Study. The basic study includes five daily readings or lessons. Each lesson combines study of Scripture with personal reflection and application (**orange** type indicates write-in-the-book questions and activities), ending with a suggestion for talking with God about what you've learned. On average you will need about twenty to thirty minutes to complete each lesson.

At the end of each week, you will find a Weekly Wrap-Up to guide you in a quick review of what you've learned. You don't want to skip this part, which you'll find to be one of the most practical tools of the study. This brief exercise will help your takeaways from the lessons to "stick," making a real and practical difference in your daily life.

When you gather with your group to review each week's material, you will watch a video, discuss what you are learning, and pray together. I encourage you to discuss the insights you are gaining and how God is working in your own life.

2. Deeper Study. If you want an even deeper study, there is an optional "Weekly Reading Plan" that will take you through the books of 1 and 2 Kings. This will give you fuller context for what was happening before and after Elijah's life and ministry. You'll find the chapters for the week listed in the margin at the beginning of each week. Feel free to read them at your convenience and pace throughout the week. Additionally, memory verses are provided for each week of study so that you may meditate on and memorize key truths from God's Word. (Though these verses relate to the specific theme of the week, not all are from the books of 1 and 2 Kings.)

3. Lighter Commitment. If you are in a season of life in which you need a lighter commitment, I encourage you to give yourself permission to do what you can. God will bless your efforts and speak to you through this study at every level of participation.

Bonus: 30 Days of Prayer for Spiritual Stamina. Whichever study option you choose (basic, deeper, or lighter), you also may want to participate in this thirty-day bonus prayer challenge—whether you make an individual commitment or your group makes the commitment together. The challenge is to spend ten extra minutes in prayer each day, utilizing a variety of prayer methods throughout the thirty days. You can find some general introductions to different prayer methods or approaches online that you can use throughout the thirty days, or if you desire the structure of daily prayer exercises, you can order a copy of *30 Days of Prayer for Spiritual Stamina* (see **www.abingdonwomen .com/Elijah** for either option). With either option, you will find instruction for praying silently, praying aloud, praying through writing, praying with movement, and praying together. The idea is that these thirty days of prayer will help you to implement what you are learning about the connection between prayer and spiritual stamina.

Take time now to pray and decide which study option is right for you, and check it below. Consider also whether you plan to do the bonus challenge.

__ **1. Basic Study**
__ **2. Deeper Study**
__ **3. Lighter Commitment: I will**_____.
__ **Bonus: 30 Days of Prayer for Spiritual Stamina**

Be sure to let someone in your group know which option(s) you have chosen so that you have some accountability and encouragement.

A Final Word

As we begin this journey together, remember that the goal is not temporary behavior modification but long-term heart change. While this will include evaluating our spiritual habits or disciplines and asking God to reveal needed changes, we want to be led by the Holy Spirit rather than our own ideas. Elijah found spiritual stamina through a close walk with God, who protected and provided for him. The Lord rewarded Elijah with His presence and peace. Like Elijah, we can find spiritual stamina in every season as we draw near to our loving God.

Introductory Background

Elijah the prophet delivered messages from God to the people of Israel. The Israelite people are descendants of the patriarchs Abraham, Isaac, and Jacob. Jacob's name was changed to Israel by God, and his descendants are the Israelite people. Jacob's son, Joseph, brought them to Egypt during a famine where they multiplied to over a million people during 430 years of slavery. God then raised up Moses to lead His people out of Egypt and into the Promised Land. Unfortunately, the people complained and rebelled and consequently had to spend 40 years wandering in the wilderness before Joshua led them into the land of promise.

After conquering the land of Canaan, God later raised up judges including Gideon and Samson, who led the Israelites in battles against their enemies. Ultimately, the people asked God for a king even though He wanted to be their king, and God gave them what they wanted. The first king was Saul. Then King David and his son Solomon ruled over Israel. These three kings ruled under what is now referred to as the United Kingdom.

After Solomon's death, his son Reheboam made some unwise choices that led to a man named Jeroboam breaking off and ruling over the ten northern tribes of Israel. This brought about the years of the Divided Kingdom. When we read the books of 1 and 2 Kings, we find the author goes back and forth in speaking about a northern king and then a southern king. The Northern Kingdom is referred to as Israel while the Southern Kingdom became known as Judah.

Jeroboam was the first of nineteen kings who ruled the northern tribes, and he set the tone for turning away from true worship of Yahweh. He set up religious places and practices according to what was most convenient for his control and power over the people, and he promoted idolatry blended into the worship of Yahweh. Every king after him in Israel was evil. In 722 BC Assyria invaded Israel and exiled them into captivity, ending the monarchy and nation itself.

In contrast, the Southern Kingdom of Judah had a few good kings. Out of the nineteen southern kings and one queen, only eight followed the Lord. (Though that number is debated, I'm including two kings who did some good and some bad, following God imperfectly.) Then in 586 BC the Southern Kingdom had a final fall and was destroyed at the hands of the Babylonians.

During the reigns of both the northern and southern kings, God always raised up prophets to call His people back into relationship with Him. This is where Elijah's ministry begins. He was one of these prophets sent by God as a mouthpiece speaking truth in a culture overrun with counterfeits.

In 1 Kings 17, Elijah issues a statement to King Ahab—the seventh king in the succession of the nineteen kings of the Northern Kingdom of Israel. Ahab's father had been a very wicked man named Omri, and Ahab not only followed his father's bad example but also exceeded it. He married Jezebel, the daughter of the Sidonian king whose land bordered the land of Israel, and she brought Baal worship to the forefront, putting her and Elijah in direct opposition. You see, Elijah's name means "Yahweh is God." His name reveals his mission. He wanted the people of Israel to turn from their sin and turn back to Yahweh.

As we explore six themes in the life of Elijah—prayer, choices, soul care, surrender, mentoring, and legacy—we will see that he was an ordinary man who did extraordinary things for God by running the marathon of life with perseverance, yielding to God, and growing in faith. He was a man who stood in the gap between God and His people— humble but bold, strong but self-controlled, questioning but faithful, prayerful but decisive. As we get to know Elijah, I pray we will get to know God on a deeper level and find the spiritual stamina we need for every season of our lives.

VIDEO VIEWER GUIDE: INTRODUCTION (OPTIONAL)

The People of Israel

The _____

Abraham

Isaac

Jacob (Israel)

Joseph

Moses

Joshua

Period of Judges, including Gideon and Samson

Kings of Israel: Saul, David, Solomon

The _____ Kingdom

Rehoboam and Jeroboam bring division

The _____ Kingdom

Northern Kingdom: _____ / Southern Kingdom: _____

Jeroboam, King of Northern Tribes—Turned People from God

722 BC—Israel Conquered

Kings of Judah—Some Good, Some Bad

586 BC—Southern Kingdom Destroyed

VIDEO VIEWER GUIDE: INTRODUCTION (OPTIONAL)

_____—Called People Back to God

Elijah—Mouthpiece of God

King _____—seventh king of Northern Kingdom

Ahab Exceeded His Father's Evil

Ahab Married _____

Queen Jezebel—Lady Macbeth of the Old Testament

Elijah—"Yahweh is my _____"

Elisha—"Yahweh _____"

Themes: prayer, choices, soul care, surrender, mentoring, legacy

"Elijah was as _____ as we are." (James 5:17 NLT)

For the prayer challenge, see **www.AbingdonWomen.com/Elijah** to find free resources or to order a copy of 30 *Days of Prayer for Spiritual Stamina*.

Week 1

Prayer

1 Kings 17

Memory Verse

And it is impossible to please God without faith. Anyone who wants to come to him must believe that God exists and that he rewards those who sincerely seek him.

(Hebrews 11:6)

DAY 1: TRUE GRIT

Weekly Reading Plan

Read 1 Kings 1-8.

Today's Scripture Focus

1 Kings 12:26-33

Have you ever felt spiritually dry? We all have seasons in our faith when we feel parched for living water. Even though we love God and have seen Him at work in our lives, sometimes He feels a million miles away. It can seem like our prayers are hitting the ceiling rather than reaching the ears of our loving, almighty God.

One of the contributing factors to my own dry seasons can be the discouragement that comes from sorting through what culture is streaming at me each day. Blogs, social media arguments, television, personal conversations, and the daily mail leave me worn out as I try to sift through all the information, which often contradicts the truths I know. This barrage of cultural messages tugs at my thoughts and emotions.

Relationships can be another source of spiritual fatigue. Let's be honest: relationships are difficult. I love my husband dearly, but I find marriage requires stamina. One day I think he is the greatest, smartest, and most handsome specimen I've ever encountered. Other days…well, let's just say I have to discipline myself to look for the good. (And he could say the same about me!)

Information overload and marriage are just two things in my world that require me to learn stamina.

What are some things that are wearing you out right now? These aren't necessarily bad or wrong things; they are simply situations, relationships, or routines that require your stamina in this season. List one or two things below:

Whether you thought of a job situation that is causing stress, a healthy eating plan you are battling to follow, or a relationship that requires some work right now, we all know what it is like to grow weary. Even great things such as church can wear us out. As a pastor's wife for more than twenty years, I love God's church, but there are some days when I get tired of the inevitable complaints, changes, and problems. I need stamina to keep loving and serving like Jesus.

Stamina is defined as "the ability to sustain prolonged physical or mental effort."[2] In our study of Elijah's life, we are going to identify some key lessons that can help us sustain prolonged *spiritual* effort. That is what spiritual stamina

Extra Insight

Elijah appears on the scene fifty-eight years after the death of King Solomon, when Israel had split into the Northern and Southern Kingdoms.[1]

is—prolonged spiritual effort or perseverance—and we need it when circumstances are good, bad, or somewhere in between. Elijah encountered seasons of waiting and seasons of action, intense opposition and incredible victory, depression and bold belief. We do too. No matter what is going on in our lives today, tomorrow, or next week, we can develop spiritual stamina in the many different seasons of life.

Angela Lee Duckworth is a teacher whose TED Talk has been viewed by millions. In it she explains that when she left her consulting job to teach math in New York City, she was astounded by how children with high intelligence didn't necessarily do well in her classes. She went to graduate school and studied predictors of academic success, and she discovered that the reason was not social intelligence, good looks, physical health, or intelligence quotients. It was grit. She defines *grit* as "passion and perseverance for very long term goals." She goes on to say that "grit is having stamina. Grit is sticking with your future—day in, day out, not just for the week, not just for the month but for years. . . . Grit is living life like it's a marathon, not a sprint."[3]

So, how do we become grittier? How do we develop stamina and help others develop it as well? We will unpack this question over the next six weeks as we study the life of Elijah, a man of true grit. My prayer is that God's Word will come alive and be active in our lives, so that our time in 1 and 2 Kings will strengthen our faith muscles and put some tangible "stamina resources" in our spiritual toolboxes.

This week we will focus on Elijah's prayers of faith and take some time to evaluate our own prayer lives. But before we delve into Elijah's prayers, we need to take some time to understand a little about Elijah's world, which was vastly different than our own. It's important to acknowledge, however, that while the government, customs, and daily life were different than ours today, the call for God's people to follow Him has remained the same.

Let's begin with the historical scene that Elijah entered. Several commentators agree that Elijah brought his message during one of the darkest hours in Israel's history.[4] The political and spiritual leaders were living contrary to God's commands, and they had drifted from the close relationship with Yahweh that their ancestors once enjoyed.

Have you ever thought that we are living in dark times? If so, what are some of the things going on in the world that discourage you?

Although Elijah lived in dark times, he found hope and spiritual stamina by offering prayers of faith. And we can do the same. Faith has always been the vehicle by which people can draw near to God in the midst of the changing seasons of life. This week our memory verse is Hebrews 11:6, which holds a great promise related to faith that we can cling to as Christ-followers.

Read Hebrews 11:6 in the margin. What promise is tucked within this verse?

And it is impossible to please God without faith. Anyone who wants to come to him must believe that God exists and that he rewards those who sincerely seek him.

(Hebrews 11:6)

How has this verse proven true in your life personally—whether in the past or present?

When we come to God in faith, we find the reward we seek: God Himself. While we can seek God in a variety of ways, prayer is a vital way the Lord has given us to connect with Him. He simply invites us to talk to Him. We won't find spiritual stamina apart from prayer.

We will explore Elijah's communication with the Lord later this week, but for now let's dig into the historical context a little more by reviewing some basic Israelite history that gives us the biblical time line:

When we come to God in faith, we find the reward we seek: God Himself.

- God revealed Himself to the patriarchs Abraham, Isaac, and Jacob.
- The sons of Jacob became the twelve tribes of Israel who left Canaan during a famine and moved to Egypt.
- The Israelites multiplied greatly in Egypt, and over time a new pharaoh enslaved the Hebrew people in an attempt to control their population.
- When the Israelites were led by Moses out of slavery in Egypt, they initially wouldn't enter the Promised Land because they feared the people living there.
- They wandered in the wilderness for forty years until Joshua led them into the Promised Land and into battle, and finally they occupied the Promised Land.
- God then raised up judges such as Samson, Deborah, Gideon, and others to lead them as they continued to fight surrounding nations to keep the land.

- Eventually, they wanted to be like the other nations around them by having a king. This began the time of the kings.
- It is during the time of the kings that Elijah's story takes place.

Read 1 Samuel 8:1-9 and briefly explain how the nation of Israel transitioned from judges to a monarchy:

God gave the people what they asked for but issued a stern warning along with it. Even with a rough start, God appointed prophets to anoint and guide the kings.

Let's look at the first three kings of Israel. List them in order below according to the following passages.

1. _____ (1 Samuel 10:1)

2. _____ (2 Samuel 5:1-5)

3. _____ (1 Kings 1:32-35)

Even though God longed to reign as king over His people, He had special relationships with those kings who sought Him in faith. As we read in Hebrews 11:6, He is a rewarder of those who seek Him. So, what kind of relationship did these first three kings have with God? Saul was overcome with jealousy and fits of anger, and he sought his own way. David made many mistakes, but Scripture refers to him as a man after God's own heart (1 Samuel 13:14). Even when David messed up, he believed God and continually looked to Him for forgiveness and help. Solomon asked God for wisdom initially but later was led astray by many wives.

These three kings ruled over what we refer to as the United Kingdom, but the kingdom would not remain united. This is why we read in First and Second Kings about different kings ruling simultaneously, because the kingdom split in two. Here's how it happened.

Major change came in the kingdom when Solomon's son Rehoboam began to lead. The people asked him to lighten the burden that Solomon had placed on them. Instead, Rehoboam threatened to increase it. So another man named Jeroboam led the ten northern tribes of Israel to rebel. Jeroboam ruled over the

Northern Kingdom of Israel while Rehoboam ruled over the Southern Kingdom of Judah and parts of Benjamin (1 Kings 12:1-20). Check out this map that shows how the kingdom was divided.

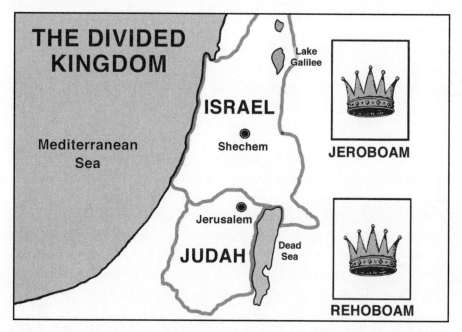

This caused Israel to be splintered into two nations. Jeroboam worried about keeping control of the people, knowing he was not a descendant of King David.

According 1 Kings 12:26-33, what did Jeroboam do to keep the people loyal to him?

How do you think this impacted the spiritual and moral climate of the nation?

Jeroboam disregarded God's clear instructions about where, how, and whom to worship. Here are some attempts he made to keep power and control:

- Made common people priests
- Moved the place of worship to make it more convenient
- Set up two golden calves

Jeroboam didn't have the grit to stay the course in following God's clear instructions. Instead, he compromised true worship to fit his preferences. One commentator observes that "Jeroboam's cult began the process of an ever-growing breach between the nation and their God, who had created them in the first place."[5]

Jeroboam put his faith in human wisdom rather than God's Word. He sought his own interests rather than closely following God's clear instructions, and His legacy of compromise filtered down to every king who ruled after Him. Not a single one led the people of Israel back to true worship of Yahweh. This outcome of Jeroboam's decisions is a reminder to us to be on guard against compromising God's Word.

Later this week we will find that Elijah sought God according to His Word and prayed according to God's prophecy and instructions. If we are to offer prayers of faith like Elijah, we must know God's Word. This drives us to seek God by studying Scripture, which involves learning the context of the original audience and then seeking to apply the principles in our modern culture. This means we must seek more information and understanding from trusted sources, ask questions, pray for wisdom, and allow the Holy Spirit to help us make application in our lives. Ultimately, we need faith to believe and then implement the truths of God's Word.

Danger comes when we compromise what we know to be God's clear instructions for our own pleasure or power. One commentator reminds us, "Whatever leads one away from clear biblical teaching about the Lord constitutes an opportunity for losing distinctive faith."[6] In other words, we must be careful that the winds of culture don't sway us away from clear biblical principles without us even realizing it. In Jeroboam's case, he didn't abolish worship of God. He simply made some small tweaks to suit his *preferences*. Yikes. That hits a little close to home for me as I think about certain areas of my life. What about you?

Are there any areas of compromise where you sense God calling you back to a more complete obedience?

What came to mind for me wasn't some big area of sin but small compromises. I struggle with things like wasting too much time on social media and television and not making prayer the priority I know it should be in my life. Making compromises in our prayer lives, study of Scripture, church involvement, and other spiritual practices can lead us down the slippery slope of disconnection from God. While we can make excuses for our lapses, we know they impact our attitudes and actions. True grit means that we guard against spiritual compromise and seek to get back on track when we falter.

Here's an important caveat. Conversations about obedience can cause us to revert into guilt and shame mode, and that certainly is not my intent here. None of us has mastered the art of obeying God fully; we all have missed the mark and are works in progress. But here's the good news: God loves us, and we don't have to perform to earn His love. When God calls us away from sin, it is not so that we can be good enough for Him. Rather, He knows that sin brings suffering, and He doesn't want us to suffer. Keeping this in mind will help us combat legalism and get to the heart of God's call to obey.

As we explore Elijah's life, I believe we will be encouraged to develop grit in our spiritual habits. We will see the power and purpose that come from growing in spiritual stamina and living the life God created us to live. Even when our nation is having a dry season in its government, economy, and cultural morality, we can flourish in faith as individuals and communities of faith as we walk closely with our God.

Talk with God

Take a moment to evaluate the level of grit in your faith. Do you tend to give up quickly, or have you developed perseverance over time? Most of us are likely somewhere between those two extremes. Ask the Lord to grow your stamina over the course of this study. Pray that your ears will be open for the truths that you need to embrace and the practices He is calling you to implement. Ask Jesus to reveal any areas of compromise so that you can stay the course of following Him in faith.

DAY 2: CALLING US BACK

I sat across from my accountability partner in our favorite little tea shop, and she asked me how I was doing. I told her with a hint of sarcasm that I was writing about stamina so, of course, I wanted to quit everything. I tried not to cry, but the tears in my eyes betrayed my inner commands to stop them. I didn't have great reasons to feel so worn out. I was just weary from parenting, meeting the demands of ministry, making another dinner, and cleaning another toilet.

We'll discover that Elijah had some weary moments, but in the midst of them he had a firm faith in the truth of his name. You see, Elijah's name means

True grit means that we guard against spiritual compromise and seek to get back on track when we falter.

Today's Scripture Focus

1 Kings 15:25-30; 16:8-33

"Yahweh is my God."[8] Elijah's name signified his mission,[9] because he spoke out against counterfeit gods and called his nation back to their Creator, *Yahweh* (Jehovah), which means the "Self-Existent One."[10] No one created God; He always has been and always will be. The unshakable truth that Yahweh is our God changes everything.

Even though life can be hard, wearing us down with all sorts of problems and pressures, the assurance that God loves us is what sustains us. His presence, purpose for our lives, and love give us stamina even when circumstances are difficult and feelings are low. We will see Elijah cling to this truth in dry seasons as well as times of victory.

Yesterday we learned that the kingdom of Israel split into two nations when Jeroboam rebelled. While the Southern Kingdom of Judah had a few good kings who followed the Lord, the Northern Kingdom of Israel had none. Unlike King David or Solomon, the kings of Israel clawed for power and authority and strayed far from God's commands.

The unshakable truth that Yahweh is our God changes everything.

Read 1 Kings 15:25-30 and 1 Kings 16:8-28, and draw a line to match each king on the left to his description on the right:

Zimri

Son of Jeroboam. Ruled two years until he was assassinated.

Baasha

Son of Ahijah, from the tribe of Issachar. He assassinated Nadab and slaughtered all the descendants of Jeroboam.

Omri

Son of Baasha. He reigned for two years until Zimri assassinated him while he was getting drunk.

Nadab

Army commander of half the royal chariots who assassinated Elah and killed Elah's entire family, including distant relatives; he reigned for only seven days and then died in a fire he set.

Elah

Army commander who replaced Zimri and fought Tibni to win the kingdom. He reigned twelve years and made Samaria the capital of Israel.

Which of these kings was described as a spiritual and God-honoring leader?

ery single one of them except Omri was
ovie.

n died in it after being betrayed.
es to protect their power.

ous leadership, King Omri stabilized the
er, the *religious* scene only went from bad
d enter.

the following:

any other king of Israel? (v. 30)

Extra Insight

Jezebel was the daughter of the king of the Sidonians.... Solomon set the example of marrying Sidonian women (1 Kings 11:1). Praised for their skillful workmanship by the ancient Greek writer Homer, they were a people committed to the worship of their god Baal and goddess Ashteroth.[12]

previous kings? King Ahab did more evil
hat if that wasn't bad enough, his choice

ing nations for mutual trade and peace
nt times. Solomon did it seven hundred
e these wives influenced him with their
b idolatry. While Solomon's wives subtly
ezebel dominated Israel with her gods
b the background as many other foreign
palace.[13] In fact, we'll discover that she
ruled the roost in the royal home and wanted the worship of Baal and Ashtoreth
to supersede if not fully replace the worship of Yahweh.

The nation of Israel had already compromised God's instructions for
worship, but Jezebel brought things to a new level of rebellion. One source
observes: "The earlier sin of Jeroboam, establishing the golden calf worship, had
been serious enough, but this introduction of the Baal cult was much worse.
It involved an outright substitution of deity as well as degrading, licentious
observances including religious prostitution."[14] These practices grieved God's
heart as He watched His chosen people trade their one true God for a myriad of
counterfeit gods who would not lead them to life and peace.

Take hold of my instructions; don't let them go. Guard them, for they are the key to life.

(Proverbs 4:13)

Extrabiblical records show Ahab was a powerful and influential ruler according to secular criteria. However, we find that God cares more about faithfulness to Him than popular measures of success. These stories compel us to consider faith and obedience as we evaluate history rather than just social, political, and economic factors.

In the world's eyes Ahab was a success, but in God's eyes he did more evil than any of his predecessors. There's a lesson here for us. We must be careful not to determine success by the standards of power, money, prestige, or dominance. Whether in our nation, churches, or families, the key to success is knowing and loving God. Elijah's name holds the key to life: "Yahweh is my God."

Read Deuteronomy 30:20 and Proverbs 4:13 in the margin. According to these verses, what is the key to life?

Loving God and following Him is the key to life. The nation of Israel got off track by determining success according to worldly pursuits and by adopting the sinful practices of surrounding nations. We can get off track, too, as culture subtly pressures us to embrace truths that go against God's Word—whether through logic, emotion, peer pressure, or situational ethics.

What are some current cultural messages we find embedded in movies, advertising, media, or everyday conversations that contradict God's way? (These may or may not be outright sins, but they are ideas that are not aligned with God's ways.)

Here are some that stand out to me:

- The person with the most toys wins.
- Revenge will make you feel better.
- A vacation is the answer to your problems.
- Life is supposed to be easy.
- Having extramarital sex has no emotional or physical consequences.
- You only live once.

While the wickedness of Ahab was extreme and Jezebel's false gods constituted clear idolatry, we can fall into more subtle forms of idol worship. When we

Loving God and following Him is the key to life.

make people, things, or power more important than God, that is idolatry. Elijah was God's voice crying out to wake the people of Israel from their reverie of sin. Idolatry beckoned God's people away from the key to life, and Elijah was God's mouthpiece to call them back. One commentator writes that Elijah "makes it his mission to teach that Yahweh lives, that Baal does not exist, and that ethical standards flow from a commitment to the living God."[15] While we may not be able to relate to Baal worship, we all battle at times to keep our commitment to God central in our lives. Yahweh is our God; He is the key to our lives.

Take a moment to evaluate your commitment to God. If He sent a prophet to your home right now, what would His message to you be? You don't have to write anything down, but take a moment to reflect, asking God if there is something you need to hear. Is there...

- a sin He would call you away from because sin brings suffering?
- an encouragement He would give you from His Word?
- a tangible reminder of His great love?

The Lord is always calling us back to relationship with Him. That's why even when His people completely turned their backs on Him with drunkenness, murder, and idolatry, Yahweh still sent a prophet to call them back. He loved them, and He never gave up on them. When it comes to His people, God is the definition of true grit. He passionately pursued the Israelites, and He passionately and persistently calls us as well, beckoning us through His Son to turn away from our sin and toward Him.

Write a sentence or phrase to summarize each verse below:

From then on Jesus began to preach, "Repent of your sins and turn to God, for the Kingdom of Heaven is near."

(Matthew 4:17)

[16]"For this is how God loved the world: He gave his one and only Son, so that everyone who believes in him will not perish but have eternal life. [17] God sent his Son into the world not to judge the world, but to save the world through him."

(John 3:16-17)

> *"When God raised up his servant, Jesus, he sent him first to you people of Israel, to bless you by turning each of you back from your sinful ways."*
>
> **(Acts 3:26)**

God used His prophets and ultimately His own Son to share His message of love. He is Yahweh, and like a good Father, He warns us in love when He sees us, His children, headed in the wrong direction. We need attentive ears to hear His words and responsive hearts to allow Him to correct our course. When you feel weary as I did with my accountability partner, cling to the fact that Yahweh is calling you back to Him. He longs to renew your heart and strength.

Talk with God

How is the Lord calling you today to turn away from sin and brokenness and toward Him? How is He drawing you close? When you lean into Him, you will find new strength. Reflect during your prayer time on these verses from Isaiah:

> *Have you never heard?*
> *Have you never understood?*
> *The Lord is the everlasting God,*
> *the Creator of all the earth.*
> *He never grows weak or weary.*
> *No one can measure the depths of his understanding.*
> *He gives power to the weak*
> *and strength to the powerless.*
> *Even youths will become weak and tired,*
> *and young men will fall in exhaustion.*
> *But those who trust in the Lord will find new strength.*
> *They will soar high on wings like eagles.*
> *They will run and not grow weary.*
> *They will walk and not faint.*
>
> (Isaiah 40:28-31)

Now ask God to reveal some tangible ways you can draw close to Him in this season of your life. Make notes in the margin if you like.

Today's Scripture Focus

1 Kings 17:1-7

DAY 3: HIDING OUT

One of the reasons we need stamina is that life often includes many seasons of waiting. The first time we took our children to a theme park, one of them commented at the end of the day that we had spent most of our day waiting in lines. However, this same child also said that the thrill of the rides had been well worth it. Following God sometimes feels like a day at a theme park. It has some exciting ups, some scary downs, and a lot of waiting in between.

I remember a season when I was waiting and wondering. About the time that our first child entered the toddler phase, my husband and I were excited to be expecting again. So, we were devastated when I had a miscarriage at seventeen weeks. We wanted to get pregnant again soon after that loss, but after eighteen months of trying, I wondered if perhaps we were going to have only one child. While I was grateful for my son, my heart longed to have more children. Those were long weeks and months of waiting, wondering, and praying.

Can you think of a time when you were in a season of waiting for something to happen?

For most of us, waiting isn't our favorite thing. Today we will find Elijah during a season when God hit the pause button in his life. He was hiding out by divine direction. Let's get into the text to discover four truths where we find common ground with the prophet Elijah.

1. *Walking with God usually includes some long seasons of waiting.*

Arthur Pink calls Elijah somewhat of a "sacred mystery."[18] This is because there is no mention of his parents, education, or really anything else about him except his hometown.

According to 1 Kings 17:1 in the margin, where was Elijah from?

Though scholars do not know the exact location of ancient Tishbe, we do know that Elijah entered the scene with an oath and a threat before King Ahab, making a life-changing prediction that affected the entire nation.

Look again at 1 Kings 17:1. What did Elijah say would not happen in Israel until he gave the word?

Extra Insight

Scholars cannot locate the town of Tishbe with certainty,[16] though one commentator suggests that Tishbe has been associated with the monastery of Mar Elias in southeast Jerusalem, overlooking Bethlehem, since Byzantine times.[17] Other Christian traditions associate the monastery of Mar Elias as a place where Elijah rested when Jezebel was chasing him.

Now Elijah, who was from Tishbe in Gilead, told King Ahab, "As surely as the Lord, the God of Israel, lives—the God I serve—there will be no dew or rain during the next few years until I give the word!"

(1 Kings 17:1)

God's heart breaks along with us when we experience difficulties, including the consequences of sin.

Elijah was commenting on a sensitive topic. In an agrarian society, rain wasn't just a picnic spoiler; it was necessary for life. Rain watered crops, and crops brought food and wealth. Warren Wiersbe has estimated that Elijah likely went to see King Ahab around the month of October. There had been no rain for six months, and he was proclaiming that no rain would fall for three years.[19] This would have been an incredible statement because the rainfall pattern was consistent and predictable, and the duration of the drought that Elijah prophesied far exceeded the occasional variances in rainfall. By prophesying a drought, Elijah was predicting a downturn in their economy, which ultimately would impede their ability to survive. Yet he wasn't making up this scenario himself. Rather, as he had sought God in faith, God had spoken to Him; and then Elijah communicated what the Lord had said.

Elijah's prophecy drove the entire nation into a season of waiting for rain. Rain was a sign of God's blessing and provision. Ultimately God would bring rain; but until Elijah gave the word, the people would have to wait. We don't like to wait. Do you ever pray about things for a week or two expecting a quick answer? We must learn to pray and wait on God's timetable rather than our own.

What are some things God has taught you during seasons of waiting?

"But be careful. Don't let your heart be deceived so that you turn away from the LORD and serve and worship other gods. If you do, the LORD's anger will burn against you. He will shut up the sky and hold back the rain, and the ground will fail to produce its harvests. Then you will quickly die in that good land the LORD is giving you."

(Deuteronomy 11:16-17)

God did bring the famine Elijah predicted, but let's not forget that, like a loving parent, God does not delight in our suffering. This brings us to our second concept.

2. *God does not delight in the consequences of sin but longs for His people to repent.*

God's heart breaks along with us when we experience difficulties, including the consequences of sin. His desire is always for us to turn from our sin and toward Him so that we might have the abundant life He wants to give us.

Long before Elijah, God had warned the Israelites about the consequences of disobedience.

According to Deuteronomy 11:16-17 in the margin, what did the Lord say would cause a famine in their land?

Yahweh wanted to remind His people that He is the rain-maker. According to Psalm 104:10-11, we know that God pours water into the streams and provides it for the animals. In Job 38:25-30, we find that God laid out the path for lightning and brings rain to the desert. He alone controls the weather on the planet He created. The Lord repeatedly told His people not to worship other gods. He even gave them the consequences in advance. I don't know if they didn't believe Him or just didn't think He would follow through. In any case, what the Lord wanted them to do was turn toward Him.

Many years before Ahab's reign when Solomon was king, God had made a promise.

Read 2 Chronicles 7:13-15 in the margin. If God were to shut up the heavens so that no rain fell, what three things did He want His people to do?

1.

2.

3.

What did God say He would do in response?

God used the famine Elijah predicted to get His people's attention because He cared about their spiritual condition. He was calling them back to Himself so that He could be a rewarder of those who would seek Him. We must be cautious not to read into Elijah's message from God, drawing the conclusion that God delights in droughts or punishments of any kind. Many verses in the breadth of Scripture support the notion that God takes no pleasure in punishment but longs for people to repent, often holding back consequences with patience as He waits for people to turn back to Him.

Read Ezekiel 33:11 and 2 Peter 3:9 in the margin, and underline the words _turn_ and _repent_. What do these verses reveal about God's heart?

While God has the power and authority to bring consequences, He does not delight in them. His heart is for us to turn toward Him and away from the

---

13"At times I might shut up the heavens so that no rain falls, or command grasshoppers to devour your crops, or send plagues among you. 14Then if my people who are called by my name will humble themselves and pray and seek my face and turn from their wicked ways, I will hear from heaven and will forgive their sins and restore their land. 15My eyes will be open and my ears attentive to every prayer made in this place."
(2 Chronicles 7:13-15)

"As surely as I live, says the Sovereign LORD, I take no pleasure in the death of wicked people. I only want them to turn from their wicked ways so they can live. Turn! Turn from your wickedness, O people of Israel! Why should you die?"
(Ezekiel 33:11)

The Lord isn't really being slow about his promise, as some people think. No, he is being patient for your sake. He does not want anyone to be destroyed, but wants everyone to repent.
(2 Peter 3:9)

harmful activities He has forbidden so that we may enjoy unhindered intimacy with Him. God clearly told His people that if they worshiped other gods, He would hold back the rain; so, He sent His prophet Elijah to let them know the timing of His follow-through.

Read 1 Kings 17:2-7, and summarize the instructions God gave to Elijah in a few sentences:

Why do you think Elijah needed to hide?

Someone recently texted me these words: "Don't shoot the messenger." Then they gave me some bad news. Ahab wanted to harm Elijah even though he was merely the messenger. God told Elijah to hide for his own protection. Hiding out doesn't always mean we are scared or in trouble. Some seasons require withdrawing in obedience. Elijah's seclusion provided time for solitude to prepare him for ministry in the years to come.

Have you ever sensed God calling you to withdraw from something or someone in obedience to Him? If so, what were some things you discovered about God or yourself during that time?

God designed us for community with other believers, but there are times when we must rely on Him alone.

God designed us for community with other believers, but there are times when we must rely on Him alone. Elijah was hidden away at the Kerith (or Cherith) Brook because he was not just prophesying hardship but challenging the gods that Queen Jezebel had brought from her Sidonian background. Though there were several Baal gods, many scholars agree that the Baal worshiped by Ahab and Jezebel was likely a storm god. Yahweh didn't delight in the earthly drought but was willing to allow temporary suffering in order to expose the counterfeits that brought graver consequences of spiritual drought.

Canaanite gods[21]	
Anath, Astarte, and Ashera	Three goddesses of fertility and war
Baal	Son of El and the god of thunder who spoke through storms
Baal Berith	A god worshiped in Shechem
Baal-Melqart	A god worshiped in Tyre
Baal Shamem	A storm god
El	Father of Baal and head of all the Canaanite gods
Mot	The god of the dead

Extra Insight

Baal is often mentioned as a fertility god, and rain-making was associated with his role of making the land fertile.[22]

3. *God supernaturally provides for the needs of* His *servants.*

Another key concept we find in Elijah's story is the supernatural provision of God. Because all of the Baal gods were associated with rain and crops in some fashion, Elijah's prophecy of a drought was an assertion that Yahweh had control of the storms, not Baal. Elijah would soon learn firsthand about God's power. After he obeyed God and walked the fifteen miles from Jezreel to the Kerith Brook,[23] he experienced God's supernatural provision while he was in hiding.

Read 1 Kings 17:4-6. How did God provide for Elijah?

God hid Elijah away where no one would find him and had ravens bring him bread and meat. Ravens were considered unclean animals, yet these were God's choice instruments in taking care of His servant. God supernaturally provided for Elijah in his time of need—even bringing him meat, which was a luxury item at that time.[24]

How has the Lord provided for you in a supernatural or unexpected way at some point in your life—whether it was a physical, spiritual, emotional, or relational need?

During my first year of marriage when we lived in Canada, we struggled financially because I wasn't allowed to earn any money while I waited for my immigration paperwork to come through. God moved the heart of a widow in our church to pay our rent on a particular month when we had no idea how we were going to pay it. She wasn't even aware of our need! God is able to supply *all* of our needs (Philippians 4:19). He doesn't promise that every whim and wish will be granted, but He does promise to provide for true needs. He has proven that to me time and time again just as He proved it to Elijah.

What are some needs that you have right now? Write a brief prayer below asking God to provide for your specific needs:

God will go to great lengths to take care of His people, providing for us emotionally, mentally, spiritually, and physically. God used ravens and the Kerith Brook to care for Elijah in his time of need. And then something happened: the brook dried up. The very famine that Elijah predicted affected him as well. This brings us to our final point.

4. Bad things happen in this fallen world, and the Lord wants to help us through each one of them.

While God provides for us and loves us, we aren't living in heaven yet. We live on a planet that has been cursed by sin, and we shouldn't be too surprised at some of earth's harsh realities. Yet things that shouldn't surprise us still can catch us off guard, can't they?

I have a tendency to freak out when the brook dries up in my life even though God has always provided for me.

- My family has never missed a meal, but when an unexpected expense comes up, I can get overwhelmed and fearful.
- We've weathered some scary health situations including septic shock, blood clots, and auto-immune disorders, but every new symptom can put me in Google-worry mode.
- Calls have come with news of car accidents, deaths of loved ones, and friends moving away, and God has been present and faithful to see us through. Still, I sometimes fear the worst when my phone rings.

- We drive old cars in our family, and there are three teenage drivers under our roof. You'd think I'd get used to car repairs, yet whenever one of the vehicles breaks down, I always seem to be shocked.

These are true confessions of someone who needs to grow in recognizing a dry brook isn't a sign of God's abandonment. It is just another symptom of living in a broken world—a world where cars break down, houses need maintenance, people get sick, and famines cause brooks to dry up.

When and how has the brook dried up in your life? In other words, God was showing up in very tangible ways, and then suddenly you couldn't see His provision anymore. If something comes to mind, write it below:

The good news is that the Lord wants to walk us through each and every challenge, just as He did for Elijah. And tomorrow we will learn more about that as we see just how Yahweh continued to supernaturally provide for Elijah's needs.

Of the four key concepts or truths we've explored today, which one resonates with you most and why?

Sometimes following God means standing alone and waiting while the brook we are drinking from goes dry, but we can trust God to take care of us. As we see Him continually show His faithfulness in our lives, we develop spiritual stamina that enables us to "freak out" less and trust Him more!

Talk with God

Spend some time evaluating what you are asking God for currently. Are they needs or wants? Do your requests have more to do with internal growth or external ease? Ask God to continue leading you in what to pray as you study His Word. Write any thoughts or new prayer requests for yourself or others in the margin.

> The Lord wants to walk us through each and every challenge, just as He did for Elijah.

Extra Insight

Zarephath is the modern city of Sarafand, Lebanon.[25]

DAY 4: CHANGING PROVIDERS

Carrie found out her breast cancer was back, and unfortunately, this time it was much more aggressive. Within a week of the diagnosis she was undergoing chemotherapy treatments. Even though God had provided faithfully through the last cancer battle, she was once again concerned about finances. They had decent insurance, but with one income and three kids at home, she knew she would need to trust God.

Her nine-year-old nephew had an idea to help raise money for her medical expenses. He loves to draw squirrels—funny, skinny, little squirrels. He asked his parents if he could set up a roadside stand on their rural lane and advertise his idea. His parents also created a Facebook page to let people know about his initiative, and he drew up a pile of squirrels in anticipation. He and his brother set up a table and waited. In about three weeks, they raised well over $5,000. The boys have been drawing squirrels as quickly as possible to keep up with the demand. They were even featured on the local morning news in their hometown. Carrie is absolutely in awe of how this innocent idea has spiraled into an international effort to show love and care for her and her family. The blessing is not only financial; it has been a faith-building lesson that will forever impact her nephews' hearts. They offered the little they had, and God has blessed and multiplied.

Carrie's family saw God provide in an unexpected way. Yesterday we saw God provide for Elijah through ravens and a brook. When the brook dried up, Elijah had a problem. He needed a new source of water. People can go weeks without food, but they will die in a matter of days without water.

Read 1 Kings 17:8-16 and summarize where God told him to go and who would provide food for him.

Where:

Who:

God sometimes sends us to places of scarcity to showcase His abundant provision.

Elijah didn't get a three-year plan for his personal provision when he spoke God's message to Ahab about the drought. As he sought God in prayer, his first instruction was to go east and hide by the Kerith Brook. The new plan was to go to Zarephath and find the widow God had instructed to feed him. Now let's explore some interesting application points in our lives regarding the *where* and the *who* in these instructions.

1. *God sometimes sends us to places of scarcity to showcase* **His abundant provision.**

We know that "Zarephath lay between Tyre and Sidon, eight miles from Sidon to the north and twelve miles from Tyre to the south."[26] Three things stick out to me about this place:

1. Sidon is a land at the heart of Baalism. God brought his prophet Elijah to defeat Baal on his home turf.
2. Jezebel was a Sidonian. The evil queen who wanted to replace worship of Yahweh with worship of Baal was from the same land where the Lord sent Elijah.
3. The widow who helped Elijah was a Sidonian. God seemed to be highlighting that He isn't against people groups as a whole. God always has cared about all people, not just those of Jewish descent. It is not ethnicity but a heart bent toward God—a heart that obeys and respects God's Word out of love for God—that separates people in God's economy. Both Elijah's enemy Jezebel and his sustainer of life were both Sidonians.

Jesus infuriated people in the synagogue when He mentioned this exact example to communicate that God's love and message were not limited to the Israelites. He said, "Certainly there were many needy widows in Israel in Elijah's time, when the heavens were closed for three and a half years, and a severe famine devastated the land. Yet Elijah was not sent to any of them. He was sent instead to a foreigner—a widow of Zarephath in the land of Sidon" (Luke 4:25-26).

God's love is for everyone, and He desires to help people find their way back to Him. Many times He uses unlikely places and people so that we won't get hung up on the mode and miss Him as the source of our provision.

> **Yesterday you considered a supernatural or unexpected way God provided for you. Let's narrow that a bit more. Has God ever used an unlikely *place* or *event* to provide for you? If something comes to mind, record it here:**

Extra Insight

Elijah had likely been at the Brook Kerith (Cherith) about one year before he went to Zarephath.[27]

God's love is for everyone, and He desires to help people find their way back to Him.

My friend Kris mentioned that she was battling depression and was pretty miserable in the small town where she lived with her husband and children. For a few months she prayed for God either to help her settle in where they were or enable them to move two hours north to a larger city, closer to extended family. Then one day her husband told her about an opportunity to move back to another state where they had lived previously. She never dreamed to ask God to move them back there, but she knew without a doubt that God had placed it on her husband's heart. It was the best thing for her family—far better than the "options" she had been presenting to God.

Though God can use us anywhere, He wants to guide us along step by step as we seek Him. Even if we find ourselves in a desolate place like Zarephath, He can provide in supernatural ways. So, God sent Elijah to an unlikely place to showcase His abundant provision. And there He used an unlikely person.

2. *God sometimes uses unlikely people to meet our needs.*

God chose to use a widow who was at the end of her rope to help Elijah.

Read 1 Kings 17:12-16 again. What did Elijah ask the widow to do? (v. 13)

How did she respond? (v. 15)

God chose to use a widow who was at the end of her rope to help Elijah. She basically said, "I'm just going to do this one last little thing and then die" (1 Kings 17:12). The nameless widow represents "the powerless, uncredentialed, disadvantaged, and hopeless" in the culture of Elijah's day.[28] What set this widow apart was her obedience to God's command. Elijah asked her to go against her maternal nature and feed a stranger before feeding her only child. Now whether or not you're a momma, you know that would require some faith in God!

I love all of God's children, but my own children have a very special place in my heart. I might give strangers leftovers, but probably not the only plate of food in the house. The widow followed Elijah's instructions in faith. She believed and was blessed.

Can you think of a time when God required an action step of faith on your part as He worked in your life? If so, describe it below:

One thing that comes to my mind is when my daughter was fifteen and really wanted a new wig. You see, she suffers from alopecia, a condition that causes hair loss, and she was completely bald. It was a special wig that cost $3,500, which wasn't in our budget at the time. I hated telling her no. The next day she asked if her dad and I would mind if she did a Facebook post with a link to a fundraising page for the wig. We both didn't like the idea at first. We didn't want to broadcast to the world that we couldn't pay for something our daughter wanted. It was humbling. The amazing thing was that in thirty-six hours the entire amount was funded! We bought the wig, and she loved wearing it.

One of the things I remember most about those days is all of the comments people posted when they contributed. A boy at my daughter's school gave twenty dollars and an encouraging word. In fact, most of the donations were small. It wasn't large amounts that funded the expensive wig so quickly but a lot of little contributions given with supportive statements that really boosted my daughter's confidence. God used the givers not only to fund the wig but also to show my daughter what an amazing community of support He had provided for her.

When the brook dried up, the Lord "changed providers" so to speak as he cared for Elijah's needs. If Elijah was my right-hand person and I was responsible for providing for him in a drought, I doubt that a poor widow would be my first thought. I would look for a rich guy with big supplies of food and water, perhaps. But as I have found to be true in the life of my own family, God often uses unlikely sources to provide for us. These unlikely sources remind us not to trust in logic or riches. God is always our source.

Watchman Nee was a church leader in China who spent thirty years in prison for his faith. He wrote about God's provision in relation to Elijah's story this way:

> Because of our proneness to look at the bucket and forget the fountain, God has frequently to change His means of supply to keep our eyes fixed on the source. So the heavens that once sent us welcome showers become as brass, the streams that refreshed us are allowed to dry up, and the ravens that brought our daily food visit us no longer; but then God surprises us by meeting our needs through a poor widow, and so we prove the marvelous resources of God.[29]

God colors outside the lines so we won't forget that He is the source of our provision.

I can certainly relate to having a proneness to look at the bucket and forget the fountain. God provides in unlikely places with unlikely people, and God changes His methods to help us remember that He is behind it all. Carrie saw God do that through her nephew's squirrel pictures. Kris saw God answer her prayer outside of the two options she brought to God. God colors outside the lines so we won't forget that He is the source of our provision.

It is not our job or a spouse's job that gives us the resources we need to live. God gave us the bodies, abilities, and resources to get us where we are today. He is the source of life. When we start trusting in the bucket, He might change it so that we can see Him as the fountain again.

This principle of the bucket and the fountain extends beyond the scope of material goods such as Elijah's food and water. God is the source of *all* we need emotionally, mentally, spiritually, and physically. We might feel that our lack is in one of these areas. Maybe a relationship with a friend, spouse, or child is a place of scarcity in your life right now.

In what area(s) do you need God to give you some reassurance or direction in regard to His provision for you?

How is the principle of God's abundant provision in our scarcity hitting home with you?

Whenever you begin to question or worry about God's provision, think of the prophet Elijah. Recall times and ways God has provided for you and others in the past. It just may be in the most unlikely places and through the most unlikely people that you see Him at work.

Talk with God

Take a moment to meditate on this verse:

And this same God who takes care of me will supply all your needs from his glorious riches, which have been given to us in Christ Jesus.

(Philippians 4:19)

Now, pray over the area(s) you listed above where you need God's reassurance or direction regarding His provision. Would you like to see a relationship restored, a marriage revived, or a bill paid? Maybe your need has to do with a job, your schedule/time, or a move to a new city. Tell God what you need. He has promised to supply it.

DAY 5: WHEN LIFE DOESN'T MAKE SENSE

A father was diagnosed with colon cancer. With a wife and three children in elementary and middle school, this was tragic news. Then his wife discovered she had breast cancer, and tests revealed it was stage four. Both cancers were terminal, meaning arrangements would need to be made for the three children who would be orphans in a matter of months or years. Dad passed away first, and his wife followed him a little over a year later. While extended family took in the children, the loss seemed overwhelming for all those around them. This is a story I know personally. Something in us grieves when we hear such tragedy. Why so much pain for one family?

It all doesn't make sense. I know there are stories that rival even this one. I bet you could write a paragraph or two recounting a story of hardship you've either lived or heard of. As we come to the last few verses of 1 Kings 17 today, we find Elijah grappling with the question of *why* when tragedy strikes around him. We will be able to relate to his struggle with honest questions but also be reminded of the power of our God.

In our previous days of study this week, we saw how God sustained Elijah with food brought by ravens and a stream of fresh water. Then after about a year, the brook dried up, and God directed Elijah to move to Zarephath, a Sidonian town steeped in Baal worship. There He guided Elijah to a destitute widow and miraculously provided for Elijah, the widow, and her son through an unending supply of flour and oil. They had enough provision for each day, and God promised to supernaturally feed them in this way until the drought ended. God changed the bucket of provision but continued to be the supernatural source.

I wonder how Elijah filled his time during those days of waiting for the famine to end. I would guess he spent much time in prayer, reflection, and solitude. This was a season of waiting and watching for him. Maybe you can relate by recalling a time when you had to slowly recover from a surgery or illness. Or perhaps you remember a time when you were anticipating something but couldn't do much except sit tight and wait on God's timing.

Today's Scripture Focus

1 Kings 17:17-24

Extra Insight

"Reared in the rugged Gilead, Elijah was a rugged individualist, a man of stern character and countenance, zealous for the Lord."[30]

Recall a season of waiting and reflection in your life, and write a phrase or two below describing it. (How did you fill your time? Did you know when the season would end?)

During some waiting seasons, I have resorted to watching Netflix and scrolling social media when I feel restless. We have so many choices to fill our time. Some things aren't inherently wrong, but if they keep us from prayer, reflection, and spiritual growth during our waiting seasons, then we won't develop the stamina we need for the trials ahead.

What are some practices that can help build spiritual stamina during a season of waiting?

Whether it is redirecting our minds, meditating on Scripture, making prayer a priority, or surrounding ourselves with the right voices, we must be intentional to prepare in seasons of waiting. Elijah spent much time waiting on God's sovereign plan to unfold. Then tragedy hit in the home where he was experiencing God's supernatural provision.

Read 1 Kings 17:17-18. What happened, and how did the boy's mom respond?

What does this reveal about her beliefs about why bad things happen?

Many people in Old Testament times believed that death and sickness were the result of some hidden sin that now had been brought to light.[31] Scripture does not support this notion. God *allows* but does not *cause* these things—and the distinction is important. We must guard ourselves from adopting the thinking of the widow of Zarephath, assuming that every tragedy in our lives is God punishing us for something we did wrong. So many passages of Scripture reassure us that God is for us. Our memory verse this week is one of them. God is a rewarder of those who seek Him. He is not out to get us. While we know that God disciplines like a good Father, He is not punitive. He loved us so much He sent His only Son to save us (John 3:16).

Now turn back to 1 Kings 17, and read verses 19-24. How did Elijah respond to the death of the widow's son?

What did he do first? (v. 19)

What did he ask God? (v. 20)

What did he do next? (v. 21)

Elijah didn't get into a discussion with the widow about cause and effect. Instead, he asked for the boy. The widow had exercised faith by feeding Elijah ahead of her child when they first met, and now she had another opportunity to trust Elijah. We don't know if Elijah had grown close to her son or what their relationship was like, but we do know that Elijah had been there for "some time" when the child died (v. 17). So, Elijah took the boy upstairs to his room and cried out to the Lord. He asked *why*.

Are you asking *why* about something in your life right now? If so, write a prayer to the Lord below, crying out to Him about whatever isn't making sense in your life or the lives of those you love:

I have cried out to the Lord many times with prayers such as these:

- Why is there so much suffering in the world, especially for children?
- Why is my daughter's hair falling out? (At times I even convinced myself that I had caused it with certain foods, stress, etc.)
- Why did my uncle, who loved God with all his heart and was such an example to so many, have to die when he did?

Elijah cried out to God with honest questions when life didn't make sense. Then he did something very bold: he prayed for the child's life to return to him.

Elijah cried out to God with honest questions when life didn't make sense.

No doubt you're familiar with other stories in Scripture of someone coming back to life after they have died. Here are some examples:

- Elijah's assistant, Elisha, raised the son of a woman who had provided for him. (2 Kings 4:35)
- A man was raised to life after touching the bones of Elisha. (2 Kings 13:21)
- Jesus resurrected a widow's son. (Luke 7:13-15)
- Jesus raised Jairus's daughter. (Matthew 9:25)
- Jesus called Lazarus out of the tomb. (John 11:43-44)
- Many were resurrected when Jesus was crucified. (Matthew 27:52-53)
- Jesus himself was raised from the dead. (Matthew 28:5-7)

While resurrections are certainly rare in the biblical record, we have heard of them. But Elijah didn't boldly ask God to restore life to this boy because he had heard stories that God had done it before. His is the very *first* story in all of Scripture where a dead person comes back to life.

Elijah asked boldly because he knew his God and believed in Him by faith. He had seen the Lord bring food with ravens. He could see a bowl of flour and a container of oil in the kitchen where he was living never being depleted. He knew that if God could do these things, then He could do anything.

By seeing God work in one area, he developed boldness to ask for something even greater. He asked God in faith to restore this child's life. But God didn't answer the first time.

Look again at 1 Kings 17:21. How many times did Elijah stretch himself out over the child and make the request?

Elijah boldly asked repeatedly until he got his answer. There have been times when I've asked for something once and then have given up when an answer didn't come. No doubt I've missed out on answers to prayer by not persisting. Perhaps you have too. More than one pastor has mused that we might find a storeroom in heaven full of all the things God wanted to give us but we never asked for in prayer.

As you consider what doesn't make sense in your life, is there a bold request you would like to make of God? It may seem unlikely, maybe

even impossible. If so, would you bravely pen the words, perhaps asking God for something you may never have dared to ask before?

I believe God can do anything. He can command ravens to feed us. He can cause oil and flour to miraculously appear. He can raise the dead. I also believe we can boldly ask Him for anything. He *invites* us to ask. In Matthew 21:21-22 we find these words of our Savior: "I tell you the truth, if you have faith and don't doubt, you can do things like this and much more. You can even say to this mountain, 'May you be lifted up and thrown into the sea,' and it will happen. You can pray for anything, and if you have faith, you will receive it."

Jesus taught much about prayer to His disciples. He used the story of a friend knocking on a neighbor's door and asking for bread to illustrate that we should ask with shameless persistence. Then he said, "And so I tell you, keep on asking, and you will receive what you ask for. Keep on seeking, and you will find. Keep on knocking, and the door will be opened to you. For everyone who asks, receives. Everyone who seeks, finds. And to everyone who knocks, the door will be opened" (Luke 11:9-10).

I wonder if you, like me, sometimes suffer from prayerlessness or wimpy prayers. We will see that Elijah's prayer life will be a great key to his faith and spiritual grit. It will be the key to ours as well. As Christians living in today's world, we could use a little more shameless persistence when it comes to prayer. So many other options vie for our attention, and prayer is certainly a discipline. It takes focus and wrestling.

Of course, we must acknowledge the mystery surrounding prayer. Some prayers are answered immediately while others are not answered for many years. Still other prayers seem to go unanswered. God chose in His divine sovereignty to heal the boy when Elijah prayed, but sometimes God chooses to wait or to answer in a different way than we expect. Even so, there may be times when we do not receive simply because we do not ask or persist in prayer.

Having said that, let's be real. Sometimes we stop asking because of the disappointment we have felt in those times when we earnestly prayed and saw little or no results. It doesn't make sense to us. In his excellent book *Prayer: Does It Make a Difference?* Phillip Yancey affirms his belief in the power of prayer to change people and circumstances while acknowledging that prayer does not follow a fixed formula, which can bring disappointment and pain:

I have a file drawer full of letters in response to a book I wrote titled *Disappointment with God*, and every so often I read through those letters. They would silence the mouth of any prosperity-gospel evangelist and break the heart of any sensitive soul. Some tell of relatively trivial unanswered prayers: for example, a baby that refused to sleep and cries louder every time the harried mother prays for relief. Some tell of unanswered prayers with more serious consequences. Scars from abuse not by bullies but by family members. A child with cystic fibrosis. A mother with severe Alzheimer's who has suddenly turned violent. Breast cancer, a brain tumor, pancreatic cancer. The correspondents give a virtual diary of prayers, begun with high hopes, buoyed by support of friends and church, dashed into disappointment.[32]

We all can relate in one way or another, can't we? For some of us, there have been times when unanswered prayer has caused us to stop praying. Others of us have continued on but with deep disappointment and confusion. We wonder why some prayers bring miraculous results, such as in Elijah's story, while others seem to lead only to disappointment. After wrestling with this question, looking to Scripture and other resources such as Phillip Yancey's excellent book, I've come to some conclusions. Here are some personal prayer concepts that I hope will help as you sort through your own questions about the mysteries of prayer:

- **We pray because Jesus told us to.** Prayer isn't a magic vending machine to ensure a life of ease and prosperity. Prayer is the way we connect with God. God desires to have a relationship with us, and so He invites us to pray.
- **When we pray, we help realign ourselves with God's kingdom.** Prayer helps us remember things of first importance and loosen our grip on lesser things and worldly distractions.
- **Prayer changes things, so we should ask boldly.** God is loving and patient, and by His very nature He desires to draw us away from sin and toward Him, opening us to His love and blessings. We do not pray to change God's mind about things—though as we see in Scripture, God responds to our humility and repentance with grace and mercy. Rather, prayer changes things most often by changing us. We pray because we know that God loves us, welcomes our prayers, and desires to be active in our lives.
- **Prayer requires perseverance.** Just because we pray doesn't mean that good things will happen. It also doesn't mean that bad things will happen. What it does mean is that as we continually seek God during

both the difficult and dry times as well as the times of peace and joy, we will develop a closeness with Him that sees us through every situation.

- **We should acknowledge the mystery that surrounds prayer.** When something goes well for us—such as a new job, a rescue from danger, or a recovery from sickness or disease—we must be careful about saying that this means God is good. What about those who don't recover or who lose a loved one or job? Was God not good to them? God is good all the time, and there is great mystery surrounding prayer. It is good to praise God at all times, and the ability to do this is a sign of spiritual maturity and stamina.

Take a moment to reread the preceding prayer points in bold, and put a start next to the one that most resonates with you in this phase of your life. Then reflect on the questions below. If you want, make a few notes in the margin.

Where is God asking you to grow in prayer?

Do you need to work through some disappointments in prayer?

Is God calling you to more boldly ask of Him and believe Him?

God invites us to cry out to Him, and I believe He cries with us in the tragedies of life. He is both compassionate and powerful. When things in life don't make sense, we have two choices: we can give in to despair, or we can continue to cry out to God with shameless persistence. I pray we will choose to cling to God in faith so that we can grow in spiritual stamina as we experience His love and peace.

Talk with God

Pour out your heart to God, asking Him for glimpses of grace in the obscurity of life.

Weekly Wrap-Up

Take a moment to review what we've studied this week. Flip back through the lessons and on the following page write an insight from each day that you would like to apply in your life. (Feel free to summarize in your own words or copy an excerpt.) I've provided an example for Day 1.

> God invites us to cry out to Him, and I believe He cries with us in the tragedies of life.

Day 1: True Grit

Example: Small compromises can lead me off track in a big way, so I need true grit to stay the course of obedience.

_____

_____

Day 2: Calling Us Back

_____

_____

Day 3: Hiding Out

_____

_____

Day 4: Changing Providers

_____

_____

Day 5: When Life Doesn't Make Sense

_____

_____

VIDEO VIEWER GUIDE: WEEK 1

1 Kings 17:1—Elijah's first words in his ministry

James 5:17—Elijah prayed earnestly for no rain

Prayer is the _____ _____ between the natural and supernatural.

James 5:16—Prayer is powerful and produces wonderful results

We can recognize the value of _____ seasons.

1 Kings 17:2-6—Elijah is in a season of being cut off

John 21:3—Peter went fishing

1 Kings 17:7—The brook dried up

God often guides through how He _____.

We must _____ in prayer even when we feel like giving up.

1 Kings 17:8-16—God provides for Elijah through a widow

Week 2

Choices

1 Kings 18:1-40

Memory Verse

Wise choices will watch over you. Understanding will keep you safe. Wisdom will save you from evil people, from those whose words are twisted.

(Proverbs 2:11-12)

DAY 1: ASSURANCE

Weekly Reading Plan

Read 1 Kings 9-15.

Today's Scripture Focus

1 Kings 18:1-15

Last week we were introduced to Elijah and found his prayers of faith vital to his spiritual stamina. He entered the pages of Scripture declaring a three-year drought according to the words the Lord had spoken to him, so we discovered that he was a man who spent time talking with God. Elijah also depended on God for basic needs and boldly called on Him when a widow's son died. We learned from his prayer life the importance of seeking God. Using our memory verse in Hebrews 11:6, we meditated on the truth that our God is a rewarder of those who seek Him. We will continue to see that truth play out this week in Elijah's life as he goes into public ministry choosing to challenge the idols of his culture.

Today we will be introduced to another follower of Yahweh serving in a very different role than Elijah. His name is Obadiah. From Obadiah and Elijah's conversation, we will discover these important truths:

- Callings from God are often varied but equally important.
- We all need assurance and encouragement from time to time.
- Sometimes we need to ask for that assurance and encouragement because people can't read our minds.

When I first began writing Bible studies, my initial audience consisted of my personal study group of about twenty women. They told me they liked my format and content. I wasn't so sure if they were just being nice or if God was really calling me to continue writing. I definitely needed assurance. God graciously sent people and opportunities to affirm the direction He wanted me to follow.

Can you think of a time when you needed assurance that you were headed in the right direction? Write below any circumstances that come to mind:

Many times I have second-guessed something I thought was the leading of the Holy Spirit in my life. Am I really supposed to go to that college? Should I pursue a friendship with that person? Is this really the best time to have a baby? God, are you leading me to this job or that city? Discerning God's voice can be tough, especially in a world with so much noise. With the constant barrage of information in addition to my own inner dialogue, I can easily second-guess myself regarding what I think God wants me to do or not do.

Extra Insight

Obadiah's name means "servant of Yahweh."[1]

Though Jewish
tradition links the
Obadiah we find in
1 Kings 18 with the
prophet Obadiah,
most commentators
agree that is unlikely.[2]
One source clarifies
that "Obadiah's
position was Ahab's
royal chamberlain,
not the prophet and
author of the biblical
book of Obadiah."[3]

Obadiah was an Israelite who felt the same need for confirmation in discerning God's leading that we often experience. He heard God's message from Elijah clearly, but he had some fears and concerns.

Read 1 Kings 18:1-8 and fill in the blanks below with the correct names:

In the third year of the drought, the Lord told _____ to tell Ahab that rain would be coming soon. (v. 1)

_____ was in charge of Ahab's palace and a devoted follower of the Lord. (v. 3)

When _____ tried to kill all of the Lord's prophets, _____ hid 100 of them in two caves. (v. 4)

_____ and _____ divided the land to search for water to save horses and mules. (vv. 5-6)

Obadiah recognized _____ coming toward him and bowed low to the ground before him. (v. 7)

Elijah instructed _____ to go tell _____ that he had arrived. (v. 8)

What do Obadiah and Elijah have in common? How are they different?

Here we learn that Elijah was not alone in following Yahweh. Hidden in the high-ranking officials of the king was another Israelite who was a devoted follower of God. Obadiah served the king and followed Yahweh behind the scenes, while Elijah boldly proclaimed God's messages and then hid away from society. For the last three years no rain had fallen, leaving the nation of Israel in a state of great famine. We are going to find that Elijah's request caused Obadiah some anxiety.

Why do you think Obadiah might have some fear about telling Ahab that Elijah had come?

This is a tense situation. Up to this point, Obadiah had been an undercover follower of Yahweh. He was devoted, but in order to keep his position he had to covertly hide priests to do God's work. Obadiah held a high government position, perhaps second only to the king.[4] Let's remember that this king was said to have been more evil than his wicked predecessors.

At first glance, Ahab seems unbelievably heartless. He and his right-hand man personally went out to look for water for animals when people were likely dying of thirst. Initially, I thought perhaps Ahab was some kind of animal lover until I realized his motivation may have been a political problem. He wasn't merely worried about his personal animals dying. In an ancient Assyrian document we find the mention "that two thousand chariots were furnished by Ahab to the Syrian coalition."[5] So Ahab needed healthy horses to draw the two thousand chariots that he had to contribute to Assyria in order to keep them from invading Israel.[6] While he may have been protecting his personal power and privilege above the welfare of his people, this was about more than animals getting fed. Ahab may have been evil, but the famine made him desperate.

I can only imagine what it was like for Obadiah to be a follower of Yahweh as Ahab's right-hand man. He likely lived with constant pressures. Obadiah reminds me of two New Testament figures who kept their relationship with Christ undercover until the right time.

Nicodemus was a Pharisee who had questions for Jesus.

According to John 3:2 in the margin, at what time of day did Nicodemus come to visit Jesus and ask Him questions?

This is the passage where Jesus explains to Nicodemus about being born again and then shares these famous words that you may know from memory: "For this is how God loved the world: He gave his one and only Son, so that everyone who believes in him will not perish but have eternal life" (John 3:16). Jesus didn't chastise Nicodemus for coming at night. Nicodemus was trying to understand the gospel by going straight to the source. He wasn't quite ready to bring any conclusions out into the open, but he was asking good questions.

Another man is listed in all four Gospels as a secret follower of Jesus.

Read John 19:38 in the margin and write below this man's name and the reason he kept his beliefs about Jesus hidden:

After dark one evening, he came to speak with Jesus. "Rabbi," he said, "we all know that God has sent you to teach us. Your miraculous signs are evidence that God is with you."
(John 3:2)

Afterward Joseph of Arimathea, who had been a secret disciple of Jesus (because he feared the Jewish leaders), asked Pilate for permission to take down Jesus' body. When Pilate gave permission, Joseph came and took the body away.
(John 19:38)

Extra Insight

There were over two thousand caves in the Mount Carmel region so Obadiah wouldn't have had trouble finding places to hide the prophets.[7]

I imagine that Obadiah had good reasons for keeping his identity as a follower of Yahweh a secret. We all may encounter a season when, as devoted followers of Jesus, we must share our faith secretly rather than outwardly.

Can you think of a time when it was more appropriate to express your faith in quiet actions rather than bold words? If so, describe it below:

Perhaps some relatives, coworkers, or friends will be more likely to understand the gospel through faithful actions than overt preaching. Of course, we do not want to make excuses for not being bold about our faith. Instead, let us genuinely seek to be led by the Holy Spirit in what will best communicate God's love to others.

Elijah was God's man serving on the front lines by proclaiming God's messages. Obadiah was God's man serving in the evil king's palace, doing what he could to save lives. In a time of drought when there was so little water that the king himself went out searching for it, Obadiah's task must not have been easy. Yet He bravely hid one hundred prophets in two caves and supplied them with food and water to save them from Queen Jezebel's death order.

Elijah had been hiding from Ahab in a faraway land, but Obadiah had been doing hidden work for God right under the king's nose. One commentator puts it this way: "Sometimes Yahweh attacks evil with the in-your-face style of Elijah (17:1), and sometimes he frustrates it by the simple subversion of an unobtrusive agent."[8] Obadiah reminds us there is a supporting cast. We tend to focus on the headliners, but God uses quiet yet crucial figures to play important roles.

We need to remember that there is not only one kind of faithful servant. Some are quiet, doing their work behind the scenes, while others are in public view. One kind is not holier than the other. We are all called to be faithful to God's instructions for us. We can spend a lot of time pointing our fingers at others who serve differently when, instead, we should be affirming and cheering one another on in our faith.

Looking to role models is good as long as we do not imitate their *actions* rather than their *faithfulness* in serving God. I like how one commentator expressed it: "Faithfulness is not so dull that it comes in only one flavor."[9] I've also heard it said this way: "You do you."

> **We need to remember that there is not only one kind of faithful servant.**

How is the Lord calling you to serve Him currently? Think of a few daily or weekly tasks that you are doing for God's glory—whether it is on the job, at home, through your church or community, or with friends and neighbors.

When I get the opportunity to meet women at retreats and events, I love to hear their stories. Some of these women are on the stage speaking or using their musical talents. Others are quietly and faithfully serving God in difficult situations. It may be that the greatest heroes in heaven won't be the well-known Christian leaders we hear about so frequently but...

- the mom who lovingly cares for her special needs child day in and day out,
- the faithful Sunday school teacher who loves and serves with joy rather than complaint,
- the single mom who puts in long hours to support her family, or
- the person who endures health challenges or relationship difficulties over long periods of time with grace and dependence on the Lord.

And that's just the beginning of a list that could be miles long, naming individuals with spiritual stamina whom most people don't applaud or perhaps even know about.

Name below a devoted follower of God who serves in a way that most people don't notice:

No matter what season we find ourselves in right now, we should seek to build up and encourage others who are living a different calling and schedule than we are. We will see that Elijah did just that for Obadiah.

Read 1 Kings 18:9-15. What does Obadiah fear will happen if he does what Elijah tells him to do?

Elijah was a bit of phantom figure, and Ahab was a scary, unstable king. Obadiah had some legitimate concerns. He read Elijah his résumé, asking for assurance that Elijah would do what he said he would do. Sometimes we need assurance too, although the approval of others should never be the guiding force of our lives.

As a habitual people-pleaser, I have a tendency to make decisions according to what I perceive will please others. The truth is that God is my audience of One, and I want to live for His glory rather than the applause of people. The Apostle Paul said in Galatians 1:10, "Obviously, I'm not trying to win the approval of people, but of God. If pleasing people were my goal, I would not be Christ's servant."

That being said, we all need encouragement. When we see someone struggling with their calling or their circumstances, we should affirm the gifts we see in them. One of the secrets to spiritual stamina is looking for the good in others and offering them specific encouragement.

Recall the person you identified who faithfully serves God even though most people do not notice (page 53). Take a moment right now to write this person an encouraging text or card, or schedule a time to call later today. Tell them that you see their spiritual stamina. Affirm the way they are devoted to God when life is difficult. Summarize your encouragement below:

I love that Obadiah expressed his concerns openly with Elijah and asked for affirmation. Too many times we stuff our fears and suffer in silence. We wish people would reach out and affirm us, but all we do is mumble inwardly or complain to others about our lack of support within the body of Christ.

Clearly Obadiah had courage enough to hide one hundred people and scrape up food and water for them in a season of famine. It reminds me of the stories of those who hid Jews during World War II, risking their lives and those of their families in order to save others. Their courage inspires us, and so does Obadiah's. God understands our fears and the need to process our faith privately before we are ready to reveal it publicly. No matter what circumstances we find ourselves in, God wants to help us grow in faith—whether undercover or out in the open.

Elijah didn't shame Obadiah or compare their callings. He didn't say, "What is your problem, Obadiah? I have been hiding out and depending on God for food provided by birds and widows! Get with the program and stop asking questions." That is not what Elijah did.

Read 1 Kings 18:15 again and summarize in your own words what Elijah said after Obadiah expressed his fears:

Elijah began by saying God's name. Some translations say the "Lord Almighty" (NIV, NLT) while others translate God's name as the "Lord of Hosts" (KJV, ESV, NASB).

Elijah was reminding Obadiah of the God they were risking everything to serve: the Lord Almighty, the Lord of Hosts. When we are scared or discouraged, we can remember the character of God and be encouraged by His power and faithfulness to help us accomplish anything He asks us to do. Obadiah confessed that he was struggling, and Elijah reminded him that they were on the same team serving a powerful God.

Are you in need of some reminders of God's faithfulness right now? If so, is there someone you can authentically share your fears with and ask for reminders of God's presence and power? Write below the name of someone who listens without judgment and points you to God:

Elijah and Obadiah had served Yahweh through a long season of standing alone, and God brought them together to remind them of the greater community of followers. Rather than be skeptical of one another, let us be supportive of our sisters and brothers in Christ.

Talk with God

Thank the Lord Almighty—the Lord of Hosts—for His great power and ability in your life. Then take time to thank Him for the gift of believers who have been supportive throughout your journey of faith. Who has encouraged you? Prayed for you? Loved you through difficult seasons?

DAY 2: SITTING ON THE FENCE

My daughter Rachel is limping as I write this. Her knee likely hurts from all the jumps and back handsprings she does as a cheerleader. The pain in her knee affects the way she walks. Sometimes I have great compassion for her, and other times I want her to do more stretching and icing to help her get better.

Limping is no fun. It calls attention to a weakness or flaw. I have stubbed my toe, banged up my shins, and had sciatic nerve pain that left me hobbling like a person twice my age. In today's passage we will find that the nation of Israel suffered from a kind of a limp of their own.

Extra Insight

Mount Carmel is south of modern Haifa, which is the third-largest city in Israel after Jerusalem and Tel Aviv.[10]

Read 1 Kings 18:16-19 and fill in the dialogue bubbles with a summary of Elijah and Ahab's conversation:

King Ahab gathered the people and the Prophets to Mount Carmel.

Ahab hadn't laid eyes on Elijah in three years and had searched everywhere trying to find him. Now they were face-to-face at last. What stands out to you in these verses about the words or actions of King Ahab and Elijah?

Ahab called Elijah the troubler or troublemaker of Israel. Ahab came at Elijah from a position of strength, calling him a name and looking down on him. Yet as soon as Elijah told Ahab to do something, he obeyed without resistance.

It is interesting that Ahab called Elijah a "troubler of Israel," because a troubler is someone who upsets peace by putting his or her own gain before the good of the community. Elijah wanted to restore the people to peace with God, which meant upsetting circumstances with a famine, while Ahab wanted to keep the peace by having no upsets in the ease of society.

Elijah said that Israel's trouble was not outer and circumstantial but inner and relational. He dug below the surface to identify the problem in his land, proclaiming that it was not the lack of rain but the people's lack of faithfulness to God.

How would you identify any outer, circumstantial trouble in your world right now? It might have to do with specific personal issues or broader issues related to work, community, or even national or global concerns?

Besides this outer, circumstantial trouble, do you have any inner, relational issues right now? How would you describe your relationship with God?

Elijah believed that the most troubling thing in life was to be far from God. Ahab was troubled by a famine that threatened his prosperity and power. What troubles us reveals what we value most.

Several commentators point out that the Hebrew word for "troubler" is the same word used in Joshua 7 to refer to a man named Achan. Achan was an idolater and liar whose death brought peace between God and the nation of Israel. Perhaps in some skewed mind-set, Ahab saw Elijah as the troubler

What troubles us reveals what we value most.

needing to be eliminated. Interestingly, though, Ahab was more like Achan in character, disobeying God's clear instructions. Like Ahab, we can turn things around so easily when we look at life without self-awareness, can't we?

Self-awareness calls us to acknowledge the difference between facts and story. Facts are indisputable statements, such as, "She walked in ten minutes late," "It rained today," or "The account is overdrawn." Story can be based on fact but isn't indisputable or provable. Story reflects our own perspectives, which can be different, such as "She doesn't value my time," "Rain makes me grumpy," or "They spend too much money."

Calling Elijah the troubler of Israel was the story Ahab wrote in his mind. We too can create stories in our minds that make us the heroines and other people the problems. We need self-awareness in order to search for different perspectives, get counsel, and be sure that we aren't missing the big picture in our situation. Otherwise, we might wind up writing a fictional story in which we make assumptions about others' motives and intents. We also might find ourselves creating a new god that isn't the God of the Bible.

In order to grow in self-awareness, we must ask questions, listen with understanding to those who are different from us, and regularly realign ourselves with the truths we find in Scripture.

As you think about the troubles in your life that you identified, how might you gain some self-awareness or see a different perspective on specific causes or issues?

One helpful self-assessment tool is to identify where you fall on the following line graph when questioned or challenged.[11]

Give it a try. Recall a recent instance when you were questioned or challenged, and ask yourself this question: *Was my response more like the words above or below the line?* **Put a check mark above or below the line to indicate your answer.**

Curious	Thoughtful	Prayerful	Listening	Humble

Defensive	Cynical	Weary	Stuck	Prideful

When we fall above the line, our spiritual stamina is evident. When we fall below the line, our spiritual stamina is waning.

Self-awareness means we are willing to hear and assess a different perspective. It doesn't mean we must accept every word spoken against us or make immediate changes, but we must be self-aware enough to process and evaluate. So, as we consider our posture toward trouble in our lives—whether it has to do with health, circumstances, or people—we need to identify those areas where we are falling below the line. In order to build spiritual stamina in every season, we must be mindful of our posture toward people and situations.

After Elijah refuted Ahab and drilled down to the real trouble in Israel, he asked Ahab to gather the people and prophets on Mount Carmel. One scholar notes that this location may have been chosen because it was on the border of Israel and Phoenicia—Queen Jezebel's hometown—and was recognized by followers of both Yahweh and Baal as a religious place.[12] Because Mount Carmel was a place that had an altar to Yahweh as well as a site for Baal worship, Elijah issued a challenge that would sort out what was real and what was fake when it came to deities.

Read 1 Kings 18:19-21, and summarize the question Elijah asked Ahab and the people:

This word picture reveals something similar to my daughter's limp. In his question, Elijah used a Hebrew idiom that "means, literally, 'hobbling upon two branches. The imagery is probably that of a bird hopping from branch to branch or a person on two crutches made of branches.'"[13] Similar to the English idiom "to sit on the fence," it is a clear call to choose between Yahweh or Baal.[14] Elijah was basically telling the people of Israel to stop sitting on the fence! Earlier in Israelite history, Joshua similarly drew a line in the sand and compelled those entering the Promised Land to choose whom they would serve: "But if you refuse to serve the LORD, then choose today whom you will serve" (Joshua 24:15).

Read Deuteronomy 30:19-20; Matthew 6:24; and James 1:5-8. Based on these verses, how does God view divided loyalties when it comes to our faith and devotion to Him?

Many times our duplicity grows not from a deliberate decision but a slow erosion of awareness. This is when we claim the name of Christ but acclimate ourselves to living contrary to His teachings. We all struggle with this hypocrisy to a certain extent, trying to reconcile our beliefs and behaviors. However, some behaviors do not coexist well with our faith. Just as worshiping Yahweh and Baal did not work for the Israelites, in the same way trying to serve both God and greed, or God and adultery, or God and bigotry does not work for us. We cannot have it both ways. Either we serve God and obey His commands or we live according to our own set of standards.

Though we all struggle to live this out, we must guard against being lukewarm as the church of Laodicea is described in the Book of Revelation. God said, "I know all the things you do, that you are neither hot nor cold. I wish that you were one or the other! But since you are like lukewarm water, neither hot nor cold, I will spit you out of my mouth!" (Revelation 3:15-16). It's an indictment of indecision—of sitting on the fence.

Walter Brueggemann wrote about the indecision of the German Christians in the days of Hitler, saying, "These were church people who thought they could live faithfully without choosing between the dominant ideology of National Socialism and the claims of Christ."[15] The truth is, we cannot waver on issues of morality. When it comes to our favorite ice cream flavor or our hairstyle, waffling is okay. But in the case of pursuing God and avoiding the sins He says destroy our souls, we cannot continue to waver between two opinions. We must choose. Elijah insisted that the land of Israel could not have it both ways, and the people fell silent when asked to decide.

Every day we make either/or choices: we will choose food that is healthy or unhealthy, we will be active or sedentary, we will scroll through social media and read about others' lives or go out and live our own, we will count our blessings or our problems, we will pray and study God's Word or we will find other things to fill our time. God calls us to make the choice to fall in love with Him. When we set our hearts and minds to love Him, the disciplines of following Him become less tiring. We find our spiritual stamina building as we choose to imitate His faith, hope, love, and forgiveness. Yet rather than try to do it on our own, we invite the Holy Spirit to do it in and through us. We choose rather than waver.

Is there an area in your life where you sense you have been wavering, dabbling in both cultural accommodation and intentional Christian community? If so, briefly describe it below:

When we set our hearts and minds to love [God], the disciplines of following Him become less tiring.

We all have areas of duplicity in our lives, but as we begin to recognize them, we then ask God to help us. Rather than sit in silence as the people of Israel did after Elijah called them to stop limping along between Baal and Yahweh, let us live what we say we believe. Though none of us is perfect, over time we will grow in faith and obedience as God's Spirit draws us more and more to Jesus' way of love.

Talk with God

Pray that you will rediscover an undivided loyalty to the God who loves you and calls you His own.

DAY 3: CHOOSING TO CHALLENGE

In Greek mythology, the Sirens were the daughters of the river god Achelous who sang songs that sailors passing by couldn't resist. They lured ships in with their beautiful voices only to crash them on the reef. In Homer's *Odyssey*, we learn that the captain Odysseus wanted to listen to the Siren song, so he instructed his men to put beeswax in their ears and tie him to the mast as they passed by the island of the Sirens. He instructed his men not to heed any motions or urgent pleas he might make for them to follow the sound.

I heard this story in a high school class, and it has stayed with me for decades. As believers in Christ, we know the promises of the world are empty. The lure of pursuing wealth, prestige, beauty, power, and selfish gain instead of kingdom priorities can be compared to the Siren song. We know that ultimately it isn't going to fulfill, but we see so many around us giving into the invitation of momentary pleasure. Just as the Siren song lulls listeners to lose the vision of where they are headed and the purpose for their travels, we can be tempted to live for counterfeits rather than God.

What are some of the Siren calls of temptation for followers of Christ today?

While culture looked radically different in Elijah's day, some things never change. Many of the lures of Baalism are comparable with the Siren calls of today. Here are four facts that might help us wrap our heads around the cultural implications of the Israelites' temptation to straddle the fence spiritually:

Today's Scripture Focus

1 Kings 18:22-24

Extra Insight

A Carmelite monastery dedicated to the remembrance of Elijah stands on the northwestern part of Mount Carmel.[16]

1. **The appeal of royal sanction.** [17] Jezebel popularized Baal worship as the religion endorsed by the crown. Worship of Baal could be likened to a certain fashion from Paris worn by the wife of the highest-ranking government official. Even if the fashion was different from past styles, a venerated public figure's endorsement and usage might entice others to embrace it as cool and desirable.

2. **Historical longevity.** Baal worship had been around since the Israelites wandered in the wilderness. Their parents and grandparents had dabbled in it. Often what one generation introduces in moderation can be taken to extremes by the next.

3. **Prosperity.** Baal was believed to have controlled the weather, which impacted crops and livelihood. The people had been convinced that worshiping and serving Baal would bring them material prosperity.

4. **Sensuality.** Baal worship incorporated sexual practices, which appealed to human desires. One commentator writes, "Baal allowed you to serve him with all your glands."[18] This appealed to the human sex drive.

Extra Insight

One of the practices that came into Israel with Jezebel's polytheism included child sacrifice. Modern archaeology reveals the practice of foundation sacrifices where infants, dead or alive, were placed in jars and put into the masonry of a building. This was meant to appease gods and ward off evil.[19]

As we put ourselves in the Israelites' shoes, can you see how Baalism offered a form of religiosity while incorporating the ability to act on fleshly impulses? If you wanted to choose a religion that felt good and made you seem spiritual, Baalism was inviting. However, the underbelly was rough. Baalism included practices such as child sacrifice and self-harm. Initially, the religion had a new, cool, and royal appeal. The real trouble was that it proved to be false, destructive, and empty. Worshiping Baal was tantamount to landing on the island of the Sirens. It drew you in like a song but ultimately led you to your doom spiritually.

In today's passage, we find Elijah fed up with the popular Baal cult that had fed God's people lies and empty promises.

Read 1 Kings 18:22-24 and complete the following:

Tally of Prophets:

For Yahweh _____   For Baal_____

Elijah commanded them to bring _____ bulls.

The prophets of Baal could choose their bull and then were instructed to:

_____ up the bull.

Lay wood on the _____ without setting _____ to it.

After Elijah did the same, what would he and the prophets of Baal take turns doing?

How would they know who the true God is?

And all the people _____.

Elijah was certainly outnumbered when he made this challenge. When you think about the contrast between Elijah and those who listened to his challenge, what detail most sticks out to you regarding Elijah's challenge?

As I read these verses, three things rose to the top that I'd like us to explore together today.

1. You are not alone.

When I taught vacation Bible school last year, a key point in one of the lessons was "You are not alone." Jesus said that He would be with us always (Matthew 28:20). I wanted these sweet students who sometimes deal with fickle friends and sad moments to know that they are never alone because God is always with them. Brady, a third-grade boy in the class who listened intently, raised his hand and said, "They should take the word *alone* out of the dictionary because God is always with us, so alone isn't even possible." I felt internal glee seeing that this kid got it! We often feel alone, but in reality we never actually are.

Elijah understood this math equation:

$$1 + God > 450 + counterfeit$$

Elijah dictated the terms of the challenge, commanding respect, and the people agreed to his plan. Later we will find Elijah very much struggling with the aloneness of his calling. We all feel alone at times. However, Brady has the right idea: because God is with us always, we are never really alone.

Fill in the blanks in the following equation with your name and a challenge you have experienced lately:

_____ + God > _____
     (your name)   (your challenge)

Now read the following verses, and put a star beside the one that resonates most strongly with you:

For the LORD *your God is living among you.*
    He is a mighty savior.
He will take delight in you with gladness.
    With his love, he will calm all your fears.
    He will rejoice over you with joyful songs.
                         (Zephaniah 3:17)

"Teach these new disciples to obey all the commands I have given you. And be sure of this: I am with you always, even to the end of the age."
                          (Matthew 28:20)

Don't love money; be satisfied with what you have. For God has said,
    "I will never fail you.
    I will never abandon you."
                          (Hebrews 13:5)

Take a moment to thank God for His presence in the midst of your challenges, and ask Him to give you eyes to see Him at work. Write your prayer in the margin, if you like.

2. Truth rises eventually.

I have to wonder if, after three long years with no rain, the people and possibly even King Ahab doubted Baal's abilities. While it would have been unpopular to say it out loud, many of the people and prophets and perhaps even the king might have secretly wondered if the Baal hype was all a crock. Jezebel's insistence on Baal's preeminence likely would have waned as the people suffered with no relief during the famine Elijah had prophesied. One commentator said it this way: "When three-and-a-half years had gone by and it had not rained, this could have meant to the people only that Baal was not living out what he was supposed to do. All this time, then, it would have become increasingly apparent that Baal was not all that Jezebel had said he was."[20] So the contest was to prove once and for all what people might already have suspected: Baal was either powerless or nonexistent.

While the siren call of counterfeits can seem to promise fulfillment, they never ultimately satisfy. Those things we trust in apart from God eventually fall apart. God is the only One who will never leave us or betray us. When we make people or things our safe places, we will be let down every time. Following God isn't always easy. Like Elijah we need stamina to stay the course when the Lord changes our buckets of provision, asks us to share His message with a resistant audience, or gives us a dream we aren't sure how to pursue.

We often lack clarity concerning the sovereign plan God is unfurling in our lives and the lives of others, but God asks us to trust Him, believing that He will prove Himself real at just the right time. One of my favorite proverbs is "The LORD directs our steps, so why try to understand everything along the way?" (Proverbs 20:24).

Elijah waited three years for God's perfect timing before making the challenge on Mount Carmel. We can learn from his example to listen and obey. God will bring the truth to light at just the right time. May we never challenge others to a truth test without first being sure we are acting on God's timetable.

Can you think of a time when you spoke the truth but it wasn't the right time? I sure can! Truth will rise in every situation. Yahweh will show Himself real whether on a mountaintop or in a valley. We must ask God's Holy Spirit to help us know when to speak up and challenge counterfeits, and when to keep our mouths shut and wait for the right time.

> **Where do you need clarity right now about whether to speak up, act, or wait? Write a one-sentence prayer below asking God for the wisdom and patience to wait on Him:**

God asks us to trust Him, believing that He will prove Himself real at just the right time.

3. God calls us to challenge counterfeits that keep us from an intimate relationship with Him.

Did you notice in today's passage the absence of Ahab? After he summoned all the people and prophets to Mount Carmel, he seemed to fade into the background. Once Elijah issued the challenge, we did not find Ahab resisting or negotiating terms. Perhaps he was watching from a distance, waiting to see what would happen. That is often what I like to do when controversy breaks

Sometimes God leads us, like Elijah, to confront the counterfeits we see in the lives of others. But more often God calls us to challenge the counterfeits that deceive and entrap us personally.

out—quietly live my life and not get too involved in challenging a counterfeit, hoping people will see it for themselves. I don't want to sound judgmental or controlling. Today Christianity seems to be known more for condemnation than grace, and I want to run far from that motif. Perhaps you can relate. Even so, sometimes God leads us, like Elijah, to confront the counterfeits we see in the lives of others. But more often God calls us to challenge the counterfeits that deceive and entrap us personally.

Take some time to reflect, asking God to reveal any counterfeits you have been clinging to lately. Consider areas that consume your time, thoughts, and money. Think of things that may distract you from God rather than draw you toward Him, and list them below:

The way to overcome idolatry is by focusing on the real thing. Take a few moments to ask God to help you challenge any temptations you are currently battling. Write a short prayer below, inviting God to have first place in your life:

Now, after challenging ourselves, we must be open to those times when God may lead us to lovingly challenge others. The key is to be sure that we are being led by God, rather than being self-righteous. And our goal should be nothing other than the hope that someone we care about will recognize the true God who loves them beyond measure. Here are a few questions we can ask ourselves before speaking up to challenge the counterfeits we see in another's life:

- What is our motive? Are we heartbroken that the counterfeit will leave the person separated from the God who loves them, or do we just want to be right?
- What is our approach? Are we depending on God's Spirit and bathing the dialogue in prayer?
- Is the timing right? What we have to say may be truth, but God's Spirit must lead us to share it on God's timetable, not ours. We must guard against emotional reactions in favor of Spirit-led responses. This usually means waiting a few hours or days to let emotions shake out.

Can you think of a situation regarding another person where asking yourself these questions might be helpful? If so, briefly describe it below:

We dare not challenge others apart from the leading of the Holy Spirit, but God always empowers us to question ourselves regarding the security we seek from things we can see, taste, touch, and feel. God alone has the power to set fire to our hearts and breathe life and purpose into the highs and lows of life. Elijah challenged counterfeits, and we must do the same.

Talk with God

Review today's three key points and circle the one you most need to hear today:

1. You are not alone.

2. Truth rises eventually.

3. God calls us to challenge counterfeits that keep us from an intimate relationship with Him.

Now ask God to remind you of His presence and truth as you rest in His divine timing.

DAY 4: BELIEVING IN SOMETHING

Lee Strobel wrote a book called *The Case for Christ*, and now there is a movie that chronicles the story of his writing of the book. As an investigative reporter for the *Chicago Tribune*, Lee believed in facts that could be proven. When it came to spiritual things, he referred to himself as an atheist. So, when his wife decided to become a Christian, he was distraught. He set out to disprove Christianity by investigating the Resurrection.

Lee researched documents and interviewed experts regarding the accuracy of the Gospels, as well as sought out authorities in the fields of medicine, behavioral psychology, and archaeology. Lee didn't trust feelings and experience, but ultimately he found that faith is needed to be an atheist as well as a follower

Today's Scripture Focus

1 Kings 18:25-35

of Jesus—or any particular set of beliefs. And he knew that he must put his faith where the evidence led. Against his own personal desires, Lee could not dispute what he learned through investigation about the claims of Christ. Eventually, he took a leap of faith and decided to become a follower of the Jesus he had tried to disprove.

All of us have spiritual questions, but in order to become Christians we must decide what we believe about Christ and the Resurrection. People like Lee may spend a lot of time in careful research while others accept what they have been taught with less fact-checking. Our modern culture often affirms believing in something spiritual yet is less tolerant of Christianity. Some people embrace the notion that the object of our belief is second to the amount of passion and personal benefit we find in our faith. Yet as we will see in Elijah's Mount Carmel challenge, the intensity of our expression of belief is useless if the object of our belief is not real.

Do you agree that passion is pointless if the object of our belief is not real? Why or why not?

Now, we should never try to force our beliefs down anyone's throat. We are to respect the differing opinions of others while enjoying the freedom to believe that there is only one true God. Still, holding to this exclusive truth can seem unkind to others. By saying that there is only one true God, the God of the Bible, we are in essence calling all other gods false. It sounds a little self-righteous; but if we really believe in the gospel of Jesus, it would be hurtful not to share with others the reality of our loving Father, Creator of all who so loved the world that He sent His Son, Jesus, to die so that everyone who believes in Him will have eternal life (John 3:16).

We share the gospel message through our actions and words and often in how we respond to our own failures or trials.

We share the gospel message through our actions and words and often in how we respond to our own failures or trials. Historically, Christians have not always done this well. There have been times when the church has used wars and witch hunts to force nonbelievers to profess Christian beliefs. Though we do not always share our faith in a winsome way, most of us share the hope that we have learned from the example of Jesus and history to *propose* rather than *impose* the gospel message. Yet even when we do not impose our beliefs on others, some may lump us in with badly behaved Christians such as those often portrayed in movies and television shows. Has that ever happened to you?

My children have struggled as Christ-followers in their public high schools. They say that sometimes it has seemed to them that every faith is encouraged and tolerated except Christianity. Other students have assumed my children were judging them when they weren't. They have had to learn how to have respectful dialogue while standing firm on certain issues.

This is a tension for us as well. Our heart's desire should be to help others come to know the one true God. Elijah did just that.

Yesterday we learned about Elijah's challenge. Summarize the gist of it below (review 1 Kings 18:22-24 if you need a refresher):

Now read 1 Kings 18:25-27, and answer the following questions:

Who did Elijah say could go first and why? (v. 25)

What was the one thing they could not do to the offering? (v. 25)

How long did they call on the name of Baal? (v. 26)

What types of things did they do to try to get Baal to answer? (v. 26)

How did Elijah mock them? (v. 27)

What are your initial thoughts regarding Elijah's insulting questions?

At first, I wondered if the taunting seemed rude or unnecessary. But as I studied, I found that Elijah might have been inciting them to their ultimate

One commentator writes that Mount Carmel could be referred to as "Baal's Bluff" because it "may well have been ground sacred to Baal, and Elijah may have chosen it for that very reason."[21]

intensity to prove that even if you believe with all your might, it does no good if the god is not real. The prevailing belief across Mesopotamia was that gods ruled over specific regions. The gods of Assyria, for example, could not be called on while in Egypt. Instead, you were to cry out to the local deity of the particular land you lived in. Elijah wanted to prove that Baal was not only limited to his region; he did not even exist at all. He challenged Baal on his own turf.

Elijah stirred up the prophets of Baal, questioning whether Baal might be daydreaming, going to the bathroom, taking a trip, or sleeping. These were likely excuses that were made when the false god didn't answer their prayers. One commentator suggests that Elijah used terms from myths about Baal that would have been known to the people.[22] Another mentions that Baal worshipers believed their god not only could die but also could "go on a journey, fall asleep, or even resort to bloody self-mutilation."[23]

In this challenge, Elijah did not want the people to make excuses for Baal's silence. So, he egged them on to get Baal to send fire. Elijah knew Baal couldn't do it, but he also knew that all of the prophets' intensity and passion needed to be expended so they wouldn't question later whether Baal would have answered if they had done this or that.

According to 1 Kings 18:28, how did the followers of Baal respond to Elijah's insults?

The worshipers of Baal were "all in" when it came to their sincerity, but they sincerely believed in a god that did not exist. Baal didn't answer. He couldn't, because he was nothing more than a made-up story, much like Homer's *Odyssey*.

We want to be sure we don't embrace counterfeits as the prophets of Baal did. Delineating fact from fiction is critical when it comes to physical health, politics, education, and spiritual beliefs. Each of these areas affects us in tangible ways on this earth. But our ability to discern spiritual truths impacts us for eternity, as well. There are many counterfeit gods in our culture today, and passion doesn't make these gods real or beneficial.

Read 1 Kings 18:30-35 and summarize Elijah's next actions:

First Elijah repaired the altar. While this site may have been "Baal's Bluff," it once had been a site where offerings were made to Yahweh. The dilapidated condition of the altar proved that the people had neglected the worship of Yahweh.

Why do you think Elijah went to such great lengths in drenching the altar?

In a time of famine, it would have been shocking to waste *any* water. But as Elijah challenged the idea of many gods with the truth that Yahweh alone reigns supreme over all the earth, perhaps he did not want anyone to later claim that fire had been hidden somewhere inside or around the altar. He wanted there to be no question in the minds of the Israelites about the matter: God is not only stronger than Baal; there is no God but Yahweh.

Here are three concepts we can take away from Elijah's challenge on Mount Carmel:

1. Beliefs impact behaviors.
2. It is possible to be sincerely wrong.
3. Sacrificial dedication to an idea doesn't make it true.

Today's lesson reminds me why we need to question, pray, study, and seek God wholeheartedly. We can so easily wander off track and find ourselves spending our time, talents, and treasures pursuing counterfeits. But God has revealed Himself to us in unmistakable ways:

- Nature (Romans 1:20; Psalm 8:3, 4)
- The Bible (2 Timothy 3:16)
- God's Spirit (1 Corinthians 2:10)
- Jesus (Matthew 11:27; Hebrews 1:1-2)

List some specific ways you have experienced God through these means in the past:

What are some practical ways you might draw nearer to God so that you have eyes to see any counterfeits that are deceiving your mind and heart?

Though it's unlikely that any of us is in danger of joining a Baal cult, we all can get sidetracked from wholehearted devotion to God. By seeking God through nature, His Word, His Spirit, and His Son, we can develop a more accurate view of God and worship Him according to His design. And as we do, we will find our God to be faithful and true in our lives.

Talk with God

Spend some time praying these verses from the psalms:

Search me, O God, and know my heart; test me and know my anxious thoughts. Point out anything in me that offends you, and lead me along the path of everlasting life.

(Psalm 139:23-34)

DAY 5: UNDENIABLE

Have you ever experienced a time when God's presence or power was so real in your life it was undeniable? I've certainly had times when my prayers seemed to be hitting the ceiling and God was silent. But I've also had moments when God's presence or handiwork was as real as it gets. When each of my children was born, the holy experience of new life coming into this world spoke loudly of another world or realm and the wonder of our Creator God. It was ludicrous to think that my husband and I could have produced this little one on our own. God's supernatural hand seemed unmistakable to us.

Other times I've experienced God in the midst of tragedy, such as the life-threatening illness of a child or the death of a dear friend. While God's power did not present itself in fire raining down from heaven, the comfort of the Holy Spirit felt near and palpable. Although we do not want to live solely by our feelings or experiences, they are a significant reality of the way God designed us.

When have you sensed God's undeniable presence or power in your life? Describe a time when you were assured that God is real and at work in the world—whether it came through circumstances, people, Scripture, church, or something else:

Today we will finish the story of Elijah's mountaintop experience when God showed up in a big way. Though God's supernatural displays are not everyday occurrences, remembering them can help us maintain the spiritual stamina to keep believing God even on the days when He seems quiet in our lives.

Yesterday we read how Elijah prepared the altar. Recap what he did after the prophets of Baal had exhausted themselves trying to get Baal to answer them:

After repairing the altar, piling wood on it, and placing a bull on top, Elijah poured water over it all—not once but three times.

Now read 1 Kings 18:36-37 to find out what Elijah did next, and write below anything that stands out to you—especially anything that contrasts the earlier pleadings of the prophets of Baal:

I'd like to highlight a few things that stood out to me. First of all, Elijah made his offering at the usual time for the evening sacrifice (v. 36). This would have been around three o'clock in the afternoon.[24] Elijah was surely following the tradition and instructions set forth by Yahweh for sacrifices. The application for us is that God is a god of order who calls us to worship Him as He prescribes rather than according to our own desires and conveniences.

The next thing that stood out to me was that Elijah identified Yahweh as the God of their ancestors. As one commentator notes, "The use of the familiar motif of the 'God of Abraham, Isaac and Jacob/Israel' was a reminder to Elijah's hearers that the covenant God of Israel is ever faithful to his people and longs to be their provider and only God in the fullest sense."[25] Elijah asked Yahweh to prove to the observers that he was the servant of the true God.

> Though God's supernatural displays are not everyday occurrences, remembering them can help us maintain the spiritual stamina to keep believing God even on the days when He seems quiet in our lives.

Finally, Elijah twice asked God to answer him. We see that both the prophets of Baal and Elijah were trying to get an answer from their deity. The Hebrew word *nh*, meaning "answer," is a key word throughout the ordeal on Mount Carmel.[26] Yet Elijah's simple prayer contrasts the long rantings of the Baal worshipers. He prayed simply, specifically, authoritatively, and briefly.

How do these four characteristics of Elijah's prayer encourage or challenge you in your own prayer life?

There wasn't any pomp and circumstance in Elijah's prayer. It was short and to the point. At times I buy into the thinking that I need a lot of time or words to pray, and it prevents me from doing it. Elijah's bold and brief prayer that brought incredible results reminds me that prayer does not require a lot of words or time. In fact, God is not a fan of empty words.

Read the following Scriptures, noting below the words, phrases, or insights from each that most strongly resonate with you:

Matthew 6:7-8

Philippians 4:6-7

James 5:13-18

From these three passages, what do you think God most wants you to understand about prayer? How can you apply this in your life?

From these three passages, I find that . . .

- we don't have to babble on and on with long prayers,
- God invites us to pray about everything,

- telling God what we need and thanking Him for what He has done will bring us peace, and
- our earnest prayers are powerful and can produce wonderful results.

As I study about prayer, I wonder why I don't want to do it more. I believe we have an enemy who knows these truths as well, and who will do anything to distract, confuse, and busy us so that prayer is not a priority in our lives. But as I'm learning through Elijah's story, spiritual stamina without prayer is impossible! We must talk to God and listen to God. This is prayer, and it is a gift that God offers to us.

Is there a specific idea or practice regarding prayer that you sense God calling you to implement?

In my own life, I have been attempting to go outside and pray for a certain amount of time each day. It requires me to say no to other things, prioritizing this practice above other tasks. Some days I fight with myself, making excuses, and others I can't wait to meet with God. Feelings are fickle, but I never walk away from a time of prayer empty. God's promise of peace is real. Circumstances may or may not change, but pouring out our hearts to God and listening to Him changes our hearts and minds.

Here are some ideas to help you think of ways you can make prayer a part of your daily routine:

- Commit to pray out loud when alone in the car.
- Set a reminder on your phone to pray at the same time each day.
- Get up ten minutes earlier each morning to spend time thanking God for who He is and what He has done and telling Him what you need.
- Ask a few prayer partners to keep you accountable in daily prayer.

What other ideas can you add to the list?

The idea is not to focus on the length of time we devote to prayer or the effort to be super spiritual, but to pay attention to opportunities to see God at work.

Spiritual stamina without prayer is impossible!

Circumstances may or may not change, but pouring out our hearts to God and listening to Him changes our hearts and minds.

Turn back to 1 Kings 18:38-39, and answer the following questions:

When did God respond to Elijah's prayer? (v. 38)

What elements were burned up? (v. 38)

What was the posture of the people when they saw it? (v. 39)

What did they say? (v. 39)

Remember that Elijah's name means "Yahweh is God." His name was his mission. Here we find the people prostrate on the ground acknowledging the truth of Elijah's name and mission. God's power and presence were undeniable!

Elijah had prayed that the people would know that Yahweh was God—and that He would bring them back to Himself. As Redeemer, God delights to restore relationships. His people had been wayward, serving Baal, a counterfeit god. God's desire was to help them find their way back to Him, and Elijah was His mouthpiece.

Read 2 Samuel 14:14 in the margin. What is the message of this verse that coincides with Elijah's view of God?

"All of us must die eventually. Our lives are like water spilled out on the ground, which cannot be gathered up again. But God does not just sweep life away; instead, he devises ways to bring us back when we have been separated from him."

(2 Samuel 14:14)

In your own times of wandering, how has God drawn you back to Him?

The Lord is ever anxious for our return to Him. God loves us and wants us to experience true power and joy, and He knows we will never find this apart from Him. On this occasion on Mount Carmel, He went to extreme measures to prove Himself as the one true God. He doesn't require begging, pleading, or religious activity, but He does ask us to turn away from sin and counterfeits and toward Him.

The last verse we will look at today may seem a little harsh compared to the previous verses about God's love for and desire to be near His people. Hang in there with me as we uncover some understanding behind it.

Read 1 Kings 18:40 in the margin. What did Elijah command after the fire fell from heaven?

Then Elijah commanded, "Seize all the prophets of Baal. Don't let a single one escape!" So the people seized them all, and Elijah took them down to the Kishon Valley and killed them there.

(1 Kings 18:40)

From our modern mind-set and cultural context, we are horrified by verses such as this; but we must remember that rebellion and apostasy were leading God's people into places worse than physical death. The influence of the prophets of Baal was bringing about spiritual death in the lives of the Israelites.

One commentator has used a story from World War II to illustrate our modern mentality toward verses such as this one. When Russian peasants helped to liberate Germany, they stayed in German homes that were unlike anything they had ever encountered in their impoverished villages. They didn't know what to do with German toilets, so they washed and peeled potatoes in them. They stared at the toilets, but they didn't get it. Likewise, when we come to passages in Scripture containing violence and murder, we can stare and not get it.[28] However, it is not for us to criticize the narrative but, instead, to seek to understand it as best we can.

Another commentator offered this insight into Elijah's command regarding the prophets of Baal: "Perhaps this execution occurs in accordance with Deut. 13:1-11, where Moses counsels Israel to purge by stoning prophets who lead the nation away from the covenant God into idolatry."[29]

No matter God's reasoning for the death of the prophets, we do not want to miss the overarching message of what we've seen in Elijah's life this week: Elijah exercised spiritual stamina and faith in God not only in a time of famine but also on a mountaintop where he experienced God's power. Through dependence on God and prayer, Elijah challenged the counterfeits of his day and brought about a spiritual victory.

Whether you find yourself in a mountaintop experience where God's presence is undeniable or at a low point where God feels a million miles away, you too can grow in spiritual stamina and faith as you continue to study, pray, and depend on God.

Extra Insight

Elijah killed the prophets of Baal in the same Kishon Valley where the judge Deborah led the people of Israel to defeat the Canaanites (Judges 4:14-16).

Talk with God

Spend some time in prayer now. It doesn't have to be an extended time. Just take a few minutes to talk to God about what you need right now. Then thank Him for what He has provided. Make some notes in the margin if you like.

Weekly Wrap-Up

Take a moment to review what we've studied this week. Flip back through the lessons and write below an insight from each day that you would like to apply in your life. (Feel free to summarize in your own words or copy an excerpt.)

Day 1: Assurance

_____

_____

Day 2: Sitting on the Fence

_____

_____

Day 3: Choosing to Challenge

_____

_____

Day 4: Believing in Something

_____

_____

Day 5: Undeniable

_____

_____

While it can seem like life is happening *to* you, God wants to work

_____ you.

1 Kings 18:16-18—Ahab calls Elijah a troublemaker

While we all struggle with consistency, God longs for us to choose Him over the

_____.

1 Kings 18:21—Elijah urges Ahab to make a choice and stop wavering

What you _____ about God greatly impacts your choices.

Hebrews 4:12-13—The Word of God is alive and powerful

_____ God's Word is one of the best choices we can make.

1 Kings 18:41-44—Elijah prays for rain

Week 3

Soul Care

1 Kings 18:41–19:18

Memory Verse

*So let's not get tired of doing what is good. At just the right time
we will reap a harvest of blessing if we don't give up.*

(Galatians 6:9)

...PECTANT PRAYER

Today's Scripture Focus

1 Kings 18:41-46

...ory of Elizabeth J. Dabney in his excellent book *The* ... 1925, Elizabeth—known as Mother Dabney—was ... in the North Philadelphia neighborhood where ...-city mission. She felt God prompting her to begin ...ar the Schuylkill River every morning at 9:00 a.m. ...with perseverance and expectation and saw lives ... She received some pushback from well-meaning ... a break from the regimen she had committed to, ... expectation even when others disagreed with her ...hen her story was written in a Christian magazine, ... letters from people who wanted to know how to

...other Dabney inspire and intrigue us because so ...h regularity and intensity. Sometimes our prayers feel wooden or rote. Other times we aren't sure how to pray or what to say. Today we will get a glimpse into Elijah's prayer pattern. Elijah prayed with expectation and believed God would do what He said He would do. In our Scripture passage today, we'll discover three key principles of prayer that can help us in our own prayer lives.

1. The Principle of a Humble Posture in Prayer

Last week we explored Elijah's mountaintop experience, when his contest with the prophets of Baal ended after Yahweh rained down fire on an altar in response to Elijah's brief but bold prayer. Now, let's see what happened next as Elijah assumed a different posture in prayer.

Read 1 Kings 18:41-46 and answer the following questions:

What did Elijah say to King Ahab? (v. 41)

What did Elijah do next? (v. 42)

Elijah prayed with expectation and believed God would do what He said He would do.

What do you notice about his posture in prayer? (v. 42)

We can learn a lot about prayer from Elijah. First, before he climbed the mountain to pray, he dealt with Ahab. He believed God was going to answer his prayer, so he communicated instructions to Ahab to prepare for rain. Try to visualize the scene. We know that Ahab had to have been nearby because after Elijah killed the prophets of Baal, he spoke to Ahab and encouraged him to go eat. I'm not sure where the king went for food, but apparently he had the equivalent of a royal food truck standing by! After all, Baal's bull would have been raw without fire, and Yahweh's bull was turned to ash. Then, while Ahab dined, Elijah climbed the mountain to look for rain clouds. I don't know about you, but I tend to picture Elijah as an old man in robes leaning on a staff, not as an agile rock climber heading up a mountain!

Once he reached the top, Elijah assumed a humble and respectful posture, and he prayed earnestly for God to do what He had promised to do. God said it would rain, and Elijah pleaded with Him in prayer to answer with rain just as He had answered with fire on Mount Carmel. Can you see him bowing low to the ground with his face between his knees? While no body posture for prayer is prescribed in Scripture, we notice that Elijah assumed a humble position and prayed fervently. He enjoyed a special relationship with God, yet he didn't forget Yahweh's holiness and power.

As you consider your own prayer life, what is your typical body posture when you pray?

Have you ever prayed while bowing, kneeling, or lying prostrate on the ground? If so, what differences have you noticed when praying in that posture as opposed to praying "on the go"?

It isn't wrong to pray while driving in a car, sitting comfortably in a chair, or taking a walk. God invites us to talk with Him anytime and anywhere without prescriptive requirements. In fact, 1 Thessalonians 5:17 says, "Never stop praying." However, we notice in Scripture that some of the times when God showed up in huge ways were preceded by prostrate prayer. Likewise, demonstrations of God's power are often followed by prostrate prayer. Last week we read in 1 Kings 18:39 that when the fire came down from heaven on Mount Carmel, the people "fell face down on the ground and cried out, 'The LORD—he is God! Yes, the LORD is God!'"

In the Bible we see that some of the greatest men and women of faith are often on their knees in prayer.

In the following verses, underline any words related to postures in prayer and circle the names of those who prayed:

When Abram was ninety-nine years old, the LORD appeared to him and said, "I am El-Shaddai—'God Almighty.' Serve me faithfully and live a blameless life. I will make a covenant with you, by which I will guarantee to give you countless descendants." At this, Abram fell face down on the ground.

(Genesis 17:1-3)

Moses and Aaron turned away from the people and went to the entrance of the Tabernacle, where they fell face down on the ground. Then the glorious presence of the LORD appeared to them.

(Numbers 20:6)

Joshua and the elders of Israel tore their clothing in dismay, threw dust on their heads, and bowed face down to the ground before the Ark of the LORD until evening.

(Joshua 7:6)

Then David said to the whole assembly, "Give praise to the LORD your God!" And the entire assembly praised the LORD, the God of their ancestors, and they bowed low and knelt before the LORD and the king.

(1 Chronicles 29:20)

He [Jesus] went on a little farther and bowed with his face to the ground, praying, "My Father! If it is possible, let this cup of suffering be taken away from me. Yet I want your will to be done, not mine."

(Matthew 26:39)

But Peter asked them all to leave the room; then he knelt and prayed.
Turning to the body he said, "Get up, Tabitha." And she opened her
eyes! When she saw Peter, she sat up!

(Acts 9:40)

At times our physical health can affect our options when it comes to prayer postures, so we must accept our limitations knowing full well that God does. Other times we can get off the couch and pray in a variety of humble postures to remind us of our position before a holy God.

As you reflect on your own personal time with God, what new prayer postures might you want to explore?

2. The Principle of Persevering in Prayer

> "History belongs to the intercessors— those who believe and pray the future into being."[2] —Walter Wink

As I've been learning about spiritual stamina in every season through Elijah's story, the importance of prayer has been a constant theme that has been hitting home with me. Walter Wink said, "History belongs to the intercessors— those who believe and pray the future into being." I want to be a prayer warrior, but many times I'm more like a prayer wimp. One of the detriments to our prayer lives can be when answers don't come instantaneously. Prayer isn't like a vending machine where we tell God what we would like and out comes the package immediately. Elijah understood the concept of persevering in prayer.

According to 1 Kings 18:43-44, how many times did Elijah send his servant to check for rain?

We find from these verses that Elijah had a servant with him. This is the first mention of someone accompanying him. I wonder who he was and how long Elijah had known him. Could he have been the widow's son whom he raised from the dead? While the Scripture doesn't tell us his identity, he plays a vital part in Elijah's persistence in prayer. Elijah kept asking even when the servant returned saying there wasn't a cloud in the sky. Elijah expected God to answer, so he continued to pray. By sending out his servant again and again, we get a glimpse that Elijah's prayer life didn't resemble a vending machine. He got six rejections before a hint of an answer came to him.

When I pray consistently for God to answer, I have a tendency to become impatient, but I have found that God doesn't work according to the microwave mentality; He is more into the Crock-Pot. He has a plan and a timetable, which means that His delay isn't necessarily a denial.

Jesus also taught about persistence in prayer.

Read Luke 11:5-11, and summarize Jesus's teaching about prayer in one sentence:

What prayer request do you feel led you to keep praying at this point in your life?

God invites us to bring our requests to Him with shameless persistence! Right now my persistent prayers are for my children to grow in faith. I'm also asking for healing for some of their physical health battles and for God to do a great work in their hearts in the midst of their struggles. Some prayer requests can be general, but God *invites* us to ask specifically for our needs.

Elijah not only prayed with shameless persistence; he expected God to answer! Recently I looked through the journal where I list the things others have asked me to pray for them, as well as the requests shared at my women's Bible study, our couples' small group, and the middle school Bible study group I facilitate. I pray over these things, but am I really *expecting* them to happen?

I have been praying for a friend's sister who is very sick. My friend is unsure of her sister's belief in the gospel, so she asked me to pray for her salvation as well as her healing. I began to pray each day for her sister. About a month later, my friend came up to me after a church service to thank me for praying. She had an opportunity to share God's love with her sister and received clear assurance of her sister's relationship with God. I have to admit that my first reaction was pleasant surprise. Though I pray knowing God hears, why am I sometimes surprised when He answers?

> God doesn't work according to the microwave mentality; He is more into the Crock-Pot.

As you think about your own recent prayer requests, whether for others or yourself, what is your level of expectation that God will answer? Circle the appropriate number.

Zero Expectation   Complete Expectation

0   1   2   3   4   5   6   7   8   9   10

Of course, we can ask for anything, but that doesn't necessarily mean it will happen. Prayer isn't one size fits all. One scholar points out that God's responses to Elijah's prayers varied. In one instance He answered Elijah immediately (1 Kings 18:36-38), while in another He answered after extended pleading (1 Kings 18:42-44a). In yet another, He refused Elijah's request altogether (1 Kings 19:4-5). The commentator writes, "We must simply live with the mystery—and allow it to teach us caution."[3] We read in the Book of Isaiah that God's thoughts are higher than ours (55:8-9). I've found this to be true in my own life. I'm glad He didn't give me back the boyfriend I begged for after we broke up in college. Other times I've asked for things that wouldn't ultimately be the best, and God mercifully said no in His divine wisdom. We can pray with greater expectation, however, when we pray according to God's Word. His promises are true.

Elijah prayed for something God had already promised. Although God spoke through prophets in Elijah's day, the promises we can pray with certainty today are found in the Bible. God's Word is full of precious promises we can cling to with bold expectation.

God's Word is full of precious promises we can cling to with bold expectation.

3. The Principle of Praying God's Word

When my daughter with alopecia lost her hair in seventh grade, desperation caused my prayer life to greatly increase. Of course, I prayed for complete and total healing. According to Jesus, we can ask for anything in His name (John 14:14). Jesus Himself asked that His suffering would be taken away, yet He also said, "Not my will, but yours" (Luke 22:42 NIV). So, following Jesus' example, I prayed relentlessly for healing as I asked for God's will, praying some of the promises of God that I knew for sure would happen.

Can you think of a time when desperation caused your prayer life to increase? If so, write below any memories or insights about your relationship with God during this time that stand out to you.

As I prayed for my daughter during her season of hair loss, I also began to pray things for her that I could cling to in prayer with absolute certainty. These are some verses that I claimed and prayed with expectation and faith:

The LORD is close to the brokenhearted;
  he rescues those whose spirits are crushed.
                              (Psalm 34:18)

"Then call on me when you are in trouble,
  and I will rescue you,
     and you will give me glory."
                              (Psalm 50:15)

You keep track of all my sorrows.
  You have collected all my tears in your bottle.
  You have recorded each one in your book.
                              (Psalm 56:8)

And it is impossible to please God without faith. Anyone who wants to come to him must believe that God exists and that he rewards those who sincerely seek him.
                              (Hebrews 11:6)

If you need wisdom, ask our generous God, and he will give it to you. He will not rebuke you for asking.

                              (James 1:5)

What other verses or promises from God's Word have you clung to in seasons of desperation or times of joy?

Of all the verses we've both listed, put a star next to the one that especially resonates with you right now. Take time right now to write the verse on a notecard or make it the screensaver on your phone or tablet. *Commit to pray this verse every day this week.*

On Day 5 we'll evaluate how this practice of praying God's Word inspired or encouraged you. Elijah prayed expectantly for rain because God had promised it. Likewise, we can pray with a posture of humility, perseverance, and confidence in God's Word and see God do amazing things.

When the servant told Elijah that he saw a small cloud in the sky, Elijah did something pretty amazing.

Turn back to 1 Kings 18:44-46, and record Elijah's response to the report of a cloud:

The report of a tiny cloud assured Elijah that a flash flood was on the horizon! Because of his faith, this small glimpse of rain was all he needed to know the answer to his prayer was on the way. God gave Elijah physical stamina on this day, equipping him with supernatural strength to run ahead of a chariot. Commentators suggest that the journey would have been around twelve miles.[4] Once again this overthrows my visual image of Elijah. Earlier we discovered the rock-climbing Elijah, and now we see that God gave him the strength to run almost a half marathon, faster than a chariot! This reminds us that God can give us physical, emotional, and mental strength when we ask and believe. Like an athletic trainer saying you can do one more repetition when your muscles are screaming "no more," God is able to provide special strength when we are running under His direction.

Moms of young children or those caring for aging parents can ask God for the physical strength and stamina to care for their families. Employees in need of new ideas can ask God for divine creativity. Those battling fear can ask God for supernatural intervention to take thoughts captive. God doesn't leave us alone to carry out the tasks He assigns us. Instead, He provides all that we need at just the right time. Let us learn from the example of Elijah to pray with the expectation that God will do amazing things!

Talk with God

Do you need to ask God for physical, emotional, or mental stamina in your life? Take some time now to pray the promise in Scripture that you are claiming this week.

Extra Insight

When Elijah ran to Jezreel, he was going to King Ahab's summer palace there.[5]

DAY 2: I'VE HAD ENOUGH

"Let's just run away." That's what I texted my friend at the end of a day filled with disappointments and frustrations. I went on to say, "I don't know where we are going or how we will live—and honestly, I know that we would never do it—but it just feels good to say it." Have you ever felt like giving up? Perhaps the drudgery of a job, the heartaches of parenting, the complications of a friendship, or just the daily frustrations of life have generated feelings that have made you want to walk away from people or responsibilities. Yet even when we utter the words "I'm just so done," we often don't mean them. We just feel that way in the moment.

Elijah knew what it felt like to want to quit. He told God, "I have had enough" (1 Kings 19:4). He wanted God to just take him to heaven. Yet God had purpose and plans for Elijah's days on earth, which included delivering messages, mentoring, and confronting counterfeits. Elijah had to learn spiritual stamina in order to keep on going when he felt like quitting.

In the verses we studied yesterday, Elijah prayed with expectation and ran with supernatural strength. Today we will find a less confident prophet.

Let's review what we've learned about Elijah's life so far. He has...

- pronounced a drought (1 Kings 17:1),
- been fed by ravens near the Kerith Brook (1 Kings 17:6),
- lived in Zarephath with a widow where there was a supernatural supply of flour and oil (1 Kings 17:14),
- raised the widow's son back to life after he died (1 Kings 17:22),
- called down fire to prove Yahweh is the one true God (1 Kings 18:38),
- killed the prophets of Baal (1 Kings 18:40),
- prayed for rain and experienced a downpour (1 Kings 18:45), and
- run with supernatural strength from Mount Carmel to Jezreel (1 Kings 18:46).

While Elijah's journey thus far has not been easy, it has included some incredible displays of God's power and provision. Yet we will see that on the heels of these spiritual high times came some low times.

I'm not sure what Elijah expected to happen after God brought fire and rain, but what would you guess he might have postulated as God's next step?

If I had been in Elijah's shoes, I might have thought Yahweh worship would be restored in Israel. I might have expected revival and a return to Israel's glory days when Yahweh guided and helped the nation as kings and priests submitted to the Lord. As God's prophet, I might have expected to have a leadership role in the revival. Though we can't get inside Elijah's head, we can surmise that the next day didn't turn out exactly as he imagined.

Extra Insight

Jezebel's name means "Where is the Baal?"[6]

According to 1 Kings 19:1-2, what happened next?

Jezebel didn't hear about the Mount Carmel contest and see the error of her ways. Her husband, King Ahab, had watched firsthand, but he didn't enforce religious changes. Instead he seemed to fear Jezebel more than the power of the one true God. This reminds us of the limitations of evidence. Even though Ahab and the people experienced the undeniable supernatural power of God, they still did not embrace Him. One commentator points out, "Sometimes Christians slip into thinking that if we only get the truth to people or press upon them our most rigorous and cogent arguments, then.... But let Jezebel be your teacher about what the human heart is like."[7] While knowledge can be powerful, only God can truly transform hearts; and our hearts must be receptive to that work within us.

God loved the world and sent His one and only Son not to judge the world but to save it. Just after we find these truths in John 3:16-17, the Scripture goes on to say that judgment comes for those who refuse to believe.

"And the judgment is based on this fact: God's light came into the world, but people loved the darkness more than the light, for their actions were evil."

(John 3:19)

According to John 3:19 in the margin, what do some people love that keeps them from faith in God?

Jezebel didn't react favorably to Ahab's firsthand account that Yahweh showed up when Baal did nothing. She responded to the evidence not with faith but with a death threat. Commentators disagree on her motives. One suggests that she sent a messenger because she was afraid to confront Elijah herself.[8] Another says that if she truly had wanted Elijah dead, she would not have warned him with a threat but would have carried it out; so, her ulterior motives were to discredit Elijah and his God before any new converts.[9] In either case, she certainly got to him.

Read 1 Kings 19:3-4, and fill in the details below regarding Elijah's response:

His emotional state:

His traveling companion:

Where he traveled all day by himself:

Where he laid down, and what he prayed for there:

What he said, specifically, to God:

What changes do you notice in Elijah compared with how you've seen him previously?

Commentators disagree in their assessment of Elijah's response. Here are some of their opinions:

- He was cowering under a threat after having seen God do great things.
- He may have taken his own importance too seriously, seeking one high experience after another.[10]
- He was running away—whether because of fatigue, fear, or a fatalistic outlook.[11] One commentator compares him to Jonah, "travelling to a far-flung place without a divine travel permit."[12]
- He saw the condition of Jezebel's heart and the reality of the situation.

Rather than see Elijah's flight as self-importance, rebellion, or lack of faith, I tend to agree with the last view—that he saw the situation as it was. One commentator writes, "Elijah was not terrified by Jezebel but broken by her unrepentant paganism and by her continuing power throughout the nation."[13]

It's interesting to note that the Hebrew verb used in 1 Kings 19:3a where we read, "Elijah was afraid and fled for his life," can have two different meanings: "is afraid," or "sees how things are." So, this verse could mean either that Elijah feared or that he saw and then retreated.[14] Both the King James Version and New King James Version use the verb *saw*, while the New Living, English Standard, New International, and New American Standard versions all translate the word *afraid*.

Whether Elijah saw the way things were going or experienced fear, he got out of town! After seeing God do miraculous things, he fled. Even if Elijah might have feared death after Jezebel's threat, I wonder if he was running from life more than he was running from death. Had he expected the battle at Mount Carmel to finally end the country's obsession with idolatry and counterfeits? Did he think that after God had proved himself by ending the drought and bringing down fire, life would drastically change for him and his people? What he found instead was one more problem to face, one more battle to fight.

When it comes to parenting, marriage, health issues, work, and ministry situations, I can relate to Elijah at times. In those moments I'm not running from death but from the constant challenges of life. You may or may not be in a low season like Elijah's right now, but we all have things in our lives that can make us grow weary.

What is something in your life that is wearing you out right now? Be honest with the Lord about it:

When it comes to _____, I've had enough, Lord.

Perhaps we would like to just "be done" when it comes to dealing with a difficult person, battling thoughts and emotions that seem to plague us, or accepting the limitations that come with health problems. I know this often happens in my life when my expectations of change or better circumstances do not pan out. The disappointment can be heartbreaking. To me, Elijah does not seem rebellious or faithless but weary and broken. We all have seasons like this in life.

Sharla wrote to me about a time when she experienced heartbreak on the heels of hopeful circumstances. Her daughter and son-in-law had tried for over two years to get pregnant. They rejoiced when their dream became a reality and they had a sweet baby girl. She was the first girl in sixty years on her husband's side, so not only were they celebrating new life but also the announcement of a baby girl. Then, when she was barely shy of three months old, the Lord called their baby girl home. She had been perfectly healthy.

Sharla shared that she was so down and depressed that at times she just wanted to quit life altogether. Her daughter and son-in-law were walking one of the toughest roads ever, and they felt much the same way. They were angry with God and could relate all too well to Elijah's statement, "I've had enough." However, they did not sit in their anger. As the days passed, Sharla and her daughter began to see the Lord's hand comforting them in totally unexpected places and ways. She said that God began teaching them to start walking one day and one moment at a time. Sharla's daughter is again expecting a baby. Even though they felt like they wanted to give up, God had plans that included "hope and a future" (Jeremiah 29:11 NIV).

Life is hard. Yet in the midst of whatever suffering or brokenness we encounter, God faithfully comforts and cares. He calls us to stay the course and work through our doubts and pain so that we can come out on the other side and see hope for the future.

How have you sensed God's comfort and presence in the midst of the brokenness in your life?

The God of all comfort shows up big when we seek Him in our moments of pain. He calls us to turn to Him when people continue to be oversensitive or judgmental, the cancer comes back, finances do not improve, or the new job is as frustrating as the old one. These and other realities of life can scare us as much as if there were a Jezebel out to get us. Elijah ran away, but God did not abandon him.

Elijah left the northern area of Israel and fled to one of the southernmost towns in Judah, Beersheba. This was the place where Abraham had built a well. Elijah left his servant there and traveled for the rest of the day into the wilderness. Some commentators suggest he was giving up on the prophetic ministry altogether. Or perhaps he was following the example of previous servants of God who went to a private place to seek God's presence.

What examples do we find in these Scriptures? Describe each briefly:

Genesis 22:4-5

Exodus 24:1-2

Abraham and Moses both had moments in their lives when they left their servants in order to face God by themselves. While it may seem that Elijah was running from God in Jonah-like fashion, it may be that, seeing the reality of his situation, he knew his need to talk with God privately and authentically in order to work through his emotions and expectations.

> The God of all comfort shows up big when we seek Him in our moments of pain.

Have you ever felt the need to get away and process the difficulties in your life? I have benefited greatly from this practice in my own life through the years. Recently I talked to a young mom who felt guilty for taking time for herself when she needed it, and I encouraged her to recognize the holiness of soul care. It isn't selfish to allow God to minister to us. Just because everyone around us is running at a haggard pace doesn't mean we should feel guilty for slowing down to ask deep questions and pour out our hearts to God. Especially when we are grieving, weary, or uncertain about the future, we should make time to run away and talk to God. We might not be able to do a day's trek into the wilderness, but we can schedule time for talking honestly with God and listening for His direction. Whether we do it alone in our room or car, at a nearby park, or in a cabin for an overnight getaway, we can seek God wholeheartedly in our moments of frustration and doubt. Though God blesses us with human relationships, none of them can replace our need for conversation with our Creator. We are to carry one another's burdens for sure (Galatians 6:2), but first we must cast all our cares upon God, for He cares for us (1 Peter 5:7).

As we continue Elijah's story, we will find that God provided some very tangible soul care for him. God will do the same for you and me. He longs to help us through our broken seasons and weary moments.

Talk with God

Spend a few moments with God sharing your true feelings about where you are in life, including serving Him. Are you weary as Elijah was in our passages today? Are you feeling full of spiritual and physical energy like the day Elijah prayed for rain and ran a half marathon with supernatural strength? Are you feeling blah with no strong emotions at all? After speaking with God about your current season, ask Him to make His presence known in your life.

Now take a moment to write below the key verse you identified yesterday to pray and meditate on this week (page 87):

DAY 3: UNDER THE BROOM TREE

Today's Scripture Focus

1 Kings 19:5-9

As I sat staring at the screen to start writing today's lesson, I felt the fatigue of the past few days wash over me. I've been living at a pretty fast pace lately. My twins are in their senior year of high school, which means college visits and extra activities. With traveling to speak, studying commentaries and writing, and the regular rhythms of dinner, laundry, and church life, I have been feeling weary and overwhelmed. One symptom of fatigue that I notice in my life is forgetfulness. I left my Bible behind in two different places recently and had to spend extra time to go back to get it, adding to my already-packed schedule. When I'm tired, I forget things, which costs me more time in the long run. Whether our schedules are full of challenging or wonderful things, lack of margin can leave us weary.

Do you ever find yourself being forgetful when you feel overwhelmed? What other symptoms do you notice in your life when you are depleted emotionally, spiritually, or physically?

In a general sense, how do physical hunger and fatigue affect you spiritually?

I posed the previous question on social media, and these are some of the answers people gave:

"I am toast. I am angry. I can't reason, much less listen to the Spirit well."

"I can't possibly focus on the spiritual when basic needs aren't met. I try hard to schedule time to rest and study God's Word so I don't get so caught up in the busyness of life that I neglect what is really important."

"I get 'hangry' and am shortsighted. I think of only the present with no consideration for anything else. My thoughts are completely absent of big picture thinking."

"If I am not focused when physically hungry, I am vulnerable to all kinds of bad decisions. But if my physical hunger has a purpose, it can intensify my focus."

Extra Insight

The white broom tree is common near Sinai where Elijah was traveling in the wilderness. It grows to a height of about ten feet.[15]

While sometimes God calls us to press on when we are tired, other times He reminds us of the importance of soul care.

These were just a few of many responses about how physical hunger and fatigue can affect us spiritually. Several women pointed out that when we are purposefully fasting from food, we can draw nearer to God through recognizing our weakness and using that time to pray and lean into God. However, today we aren't referring to fasting for intentional focus on God. We are talking about those times when we are tired or hungry due to the season of life or circumstance.

God is tender and compassionate when we are weary. While sometimes God calls us to press on when we are tired, other times He reminds us of the importance of soul care. Soul care is vital to our spiritual stamina. We are not like the Energizer Bunny. We need to stop and take breaks. Rest is a gift God gives us, but we must accept that gift. In order to gain spiritual stamina, we must recognize our unique symptoms that remind us of our need to rest and restore. Especially when we come off seasons when we have been running hard through spiritual highs or lows, we need our own "broom tree" like Elijah found on his trek through the wilderness.

Read 1 Kings 19:4-5. After Elijah sat and prayed, he did something important. What was it?

Elijah slept. I am not a regular napper. I try to get adequate sleep at night and plow through my days without napping. Not everyone is wired with the same sleep needs, but we all do require it.

What are your typical patterns of sleep? Note anything positive about your sleep habits as well as sleep challenges you have been experiencing lately:

Healthy sleep habits:

Sleep challenges:

Read the following verses, and write any insights or reminders you find regarding God and sleep:

"But you, O Lord, are a shield around me; you are my glory, the one who holds my head high. I cried out to the Lord, and he answered me from his holy mountain. I lay down and slept, yet I woke up in safety, for the Lord was watching over me.

(Psalm 3:3-5)

I look up to the mountains—does my help come from there? My help comes from the Lord, who made heaven and earth! He will not let you stumble; the one who watches over you will not slumber. Indeed, he who watches over Israel never slumbers or sleeps.

(Psalm 121:1-4)

Insights regarding God and sleep:

God never sleeps, but He watches over us when we sleep. I notice in these psalms a connection between sleep and seasons of crying out to God for help. Like the writers of these psalms, Elijah poured out his brokenness to God. He even voiced his desire to die during this season of spiritual, emotional, mental, and physical fatigue. Yet if he truly had wanted to leave life on earth, he simply could have stayed in Jezreel. Queen Jezebel had threatened to kill him, so sticking around would have been a sure path to death. Instead, he ran away and expressed his overwhelming feelings to Yahweh.

Elijah had had enough of people worshiping false gods and living contrary to God's instructions. Having been in hiding for over three years during the famine, he might have been looking forward to not living on the run anymore. Yet he knew that Jezebel's message meant more running and hiding. So, he told God exactly how he felt in a prayer under a broom tree.

Elijah's fatigue and dramatic statements did not garner him a sermon from God. Instead, Yahweh sent an angel to wake Elijah and offer supernatural provisions of food.

Read 1 Kings 19:6-9, and complete the time line below with words or simple drawings:

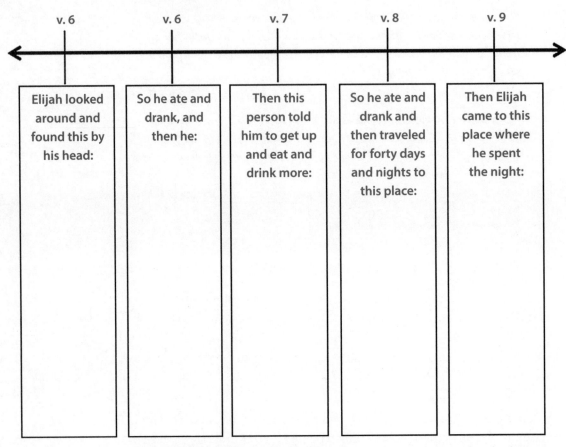

v. 6	v. 6	v. 7	v. 8	v. 9
Elijah looked around and found this by his head:	So he ate and drank, and then he:	Then this person told him to get up and eat and drink more:	So he ate and drank and then traveled for forty days and nights to this place:	Then Elijah came to this place where he spent the night:

Elijah needed food and rest, and God provided for him under the broom tree. The God that Elijah worshiped was the God of Abraham. You may remember that when Abraham offered his son Isaac to the Lord, God provided a ram instead. Then Abraham recited a name for Yahweh that Elijah came to understand firsthand as well.

Abraham named the place Yahweh-Yireh (which means "the Lord will provide"). To this day, people still use that name as a proverb: "On the mountain of the Lord it will be provided." (Genesis 22:14)

Read Genesis 22:14 in the margin, and write below this name of God and its meaning:

Yahweh is a provider by nature. He provided for Elijah's needs and then sent Elijah to Mount Sinai to show Himself to him.

List the ways God has provided for Elijah—and those he represented—up to this point. (See 1 Kings 17:6; 17:16; 17:22; 18:37-38; 18:42-46.)

With ravens, a brook, a widow, fire, and rain, God had met both physical and spiritual needs. He had proven Himself over and over as a God who would take care of His messenger.

How have you witnessed God's provision in your life? Try to list at least three ways you've seen God provide for you or loved ones whether physically, emotionally, mentally, or spiritually.

1.

2.

3.

God has provided for me financially in specific ways. In college my car needed repairs and my parents were serving overseas at the time as missionaries. I checked my mailbox and found a check with the exact amount for the repairs and a note from my uncle, saying that the Lord had moved him to send it. Other times the Lord has provided physical strength to teach or serve when I felt weary. Even though I still struggle with doubt when new problems arise, I have seen God supernaturally provide for me many times in a variety of ways. Elijah saw God at work in the past, but he needed constant reminders of God's help. We too must look to the Lord continually for present needs even though we've seen Him work in the past.

What are some present needs that you are praying about in your life right now?

Perhaps, like Elijah, you have a need for sleep and healthy, restorative food. Maybe your needs are for provisions such as a home, car, or an income to pay the bills. Or perhaps your needs have to do with a relationship or emotional challenges in your life at the present. God is Yahweh Yireh. He provided for Abraham and Elijah, and He will provide for us too.

A secret to spiritual stamina: We must consider our physical needs as part of our spiritual health.

God's angelic provision may have reminded Elijah of God's care for him at the Kerith Brook and the town of Zarephath. Before Elijah could hear God and receive guidance, he needed physical restoration. At this point he didn't need another message, event, or person. What he needed was simply to sleep and eat. God knew this and used an angel to supernaturally meet Elijah's needs. We learn from Elijah's story a secret to spiritual stamina: We must consider our physical needs as part of our spiritual health.

Perhaps you are resonating with the need for better physical care, or you may be feeling satisfied and well rested right now. In either case, a huge part of having spiritual stamina is being prepared for the changing seasons of our lives. One of my friends shared an acronym she learned in a twelve-step program that is helpful when it comes to being mindful of our physical and spiritual states: HALT. We all can benefit from the wisdom in these letters that serve as signals that it is time to stop and engage in some soul care:

H Hungry
A Angry
L Lonely
T Tired

In these states, it can be difficult to remember what we know to be true about God and ourselves. Jesus faced seasons when He felt some of these things. In the wilderness of preparation where he spent forty days before He began His earthly ministry, Jesus fasted. This was when the devil came to tempt Him. Our enemy doesn't have many new tricks. He often uses our physically weak times to accuse or tempt us. But as we see in Jesus' example, we can overcome him with God's Word and power.

> **Do you have any HALT symptoms in your life today? If so, what types of soul care might God be calling you to engage in regarding these symptoms this week?**

Perhaps you need to schedule a massage, have a nap, or take a break from a responsibility that has you overextended physically or emotionally. We can learn from Elijah that there is a season to just sleep and eat with no guilt. Ecclesiastes 3:1 says, "For everything there is a season, a time for every activity under heaven." We don't live our entire lives under the broom tree, but we have seasons where we can't go on to do God's work without some restorative soul care.

Even amazing victories such as those Elijah experienced on the mountain-top can leave us depleted. And when we are tired and hungry, our fears and doubts can multiply. Elijah slept and ate and drank. Then he slept some more and ate and drank again. Elijah needed the strength to travel to Mount Sinai. We too need restorative time for soul care to prepare us for the journey ahead. Whether our travels are geographical or mental and emotional, we all need times of rest.

I wonder if the Lord may be calling you to a "broom tree" in the midst of a busy season right now. This can seem impossible during some times in our lives. I remember being diagnosed with mononucleosis when my twins were toddlers and my son was four years old. The doctor said I needed to spend a week in bed in order to recover. I looked at this young doctor and asked if she had kids. It seemed impossible for me to spend time resting with no family close by to help with the kids. Regrettably, I pressed through with many tears and a martyr attitude rather than ask anyone for help.

Looking back, I realize I needed a "broom tree." I could have at least tried to make arrangements and asked for help. My pride and desire to manage life all by myself left me literally sick and tired. It can be especially challenging to rest when we are caring for children, doing shift work, working long hours, grieving loss, or enduring a season of life that is placing great demands on our time and emotions. It is my prayer that in these seasons, as well as in the everyday flow of our lives, we will ask for help and not feel guilty for finding rest and renewal under a "broom tree."

Talk with God

Ask God for practical wisdom regarding your sleeping and eating habits. If you are in need of a "broom tree," ask God to show it to you. Take time once again to review and pray the promise verse you have selected (page 87), and continue to cling to this promise of God as you care for your soul this week!

DAY 4: IN THE WHISPER

Last summer I took my daughter on an overnight outing as we worked through a resource called *Passport2Identity*, which includes messages designed for fourteen- to seventeen-year-old girls and their moms to listen to together. One of the clips was a message from author and speaker Francis Chan, who spoke to high school students about the sex trafficking trade in Thailand and

We need restorative time for soul care to prepare us for the journey ahead.

Today's Scripture Focus

1 Kings 19:9-13

Extra Insight

"The forty days and forty nights marks a long time and identifies Elijah as a second Moses...just as it did Christ." (See Exodus 24:18; 34:28; Deuteronomy 9:8-10; and Matthew 4:2.)[16]

asked who would be willing to go with him to help rescue children. He warned the students that they could lose their lives because of the dangers. Many students raised their hands, saying they would be willing to die in the service of Christ. Then he challenged them, asking that if they were willing to *die* for Christ, would they be willing to *live* for Him. He said that God calls all disciples to study the Bible, pray, and share their faith with others. He then asked if they were willing to do something spectacular for God, would they also be willing to do what seems ordinary for Him.

This question resonated with both my daughter and me. I often want to see God work in remarkable ways, but I am not always willing to obey Him in the small, unremarkable instructions. Jesus said it this way, "If you are faithful in little things, you will be faithful in large ones" (Luke 16:10a).

So far in our study of Elijah's life and ministry, we have witnessed the God of the spectacular. He brought famine, fire, and rain; then He patiently listened to Elijah's desire to give up before miraculously providing for his needs. In our text today, we will find a reminder that God often speaks in the whisper rather than in the spectacular.

Read 1 Kings 19:8-13, and write a brief summary of what happened in your own words:

God used Elijah's rejuvenation under the broom tree to prepare him for forty days of travel in the wilderness. Both Moses and Jesus also spent forty days in the wilderness communing with God and preparing for ministry. At the end of Elijah's trek, he reached Mount Sinai, which was referred to as the "mountain of God." One commentator suggests that the cave mentioned here might have been the same cleft of the rock where God had placed Moses when His glory passed by (Exodus 33:21-23).[17]

I can't imagine being on any kind of journey without human contact for forty days. I wonder where my thoughts would roam and if I would talk out loud at times just so I wouldn't get out of practice. The concept is so foreign to our connected culture that we need a moment to try to understand Elijah's frame of mind.

Take a moment to consider what it would be like to interrupt your life and trek through a wilderness alone for forty days. Imagine no cell

phones, no social media or email, no human contact. Describe what you think that would be like:

I don't know if the food the angel provided under the broom tree was enough that Elijah didn't eat for these forty days, but he would have had to look for water and shelter in which to sleep. When he finally reached the cave, God asked Him a question.

Look again at 1 Kings 19:9. What was this question?

Commentators disagree regarding God's tone. Some see this question as a rebuke, while others see this as God asking Elijah to reflect on how he got here.

As you consider the context surrounding this verse and the character of God, what are your thoughts regarding this question that God asked of Elijah?

God is the perfect counselor. When I've been to counselors for help in challenging seasons in my marriage and parenting, I have benefited from some helpful suggestions, but even more from good questions that help me remember truths I know and apply them to real life. Proverbs 20:5 says, "Though good advice lies deep within the heart, a person with understanding will draw it out." I wonder if Yahweh was drawing out wisdom from Elijah so that he could process his fears and faith.

Review 1 Kings 19:10, and complete Elijah's three-part response to Yahweh's question:

1. I have done this:

2. The people of Israel have done this:

3. I am the only prophet left, and now they are trying to do this to me:

What kind of tone do you sense in Elijah's answer?

While we must be careful not to read anything into the text, Elijah does seem to be in a bit of a "woe is me" frame of mind. One commentator said it this way, "His soul was somewhat bitter at having served God so earnestly and spectacularly and yet having experienced rejection and solitary exile."[18]

Elijah stated the facts. All of his reasons were true. The convicting portion of this for me is that he was upset for God's sake, not his own. He was upset that the people continued to worship counterfeit gods and had killed God's servants. He wasn't complaining about the difficult circumstances of his life. My "woe is me" scenarios are typically more personal than corporate.

Elijah was grieved that his own people had abandoned their God, and in the midst of his discouragement and frustration, God once again did not preach at him or rebuke him. Instead, Yahweh reminded Elijah of the God he served by revealing more of Himself to Elijah.

Review 1 Kings 19:11-12a. What did God instruct Elijah to do?

In the circles below, draw or describe the three spectacular displays that God revealed to Elijah:

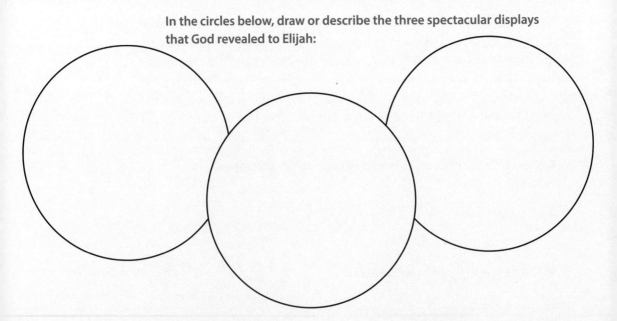

God was not in any of these spectacular displays. Instead, how did God speak to Elijah according to 1 Kings 19:12b-13?

There is some debate as to the Hebrew translation of "gentle whisper." Your translation may use:

- a sound of sheer silence (NRSV)
- a gentle blowing (NASB)
- a gentle whisper (NIV)
- a gentle breeze (CEV)
- a still small voice (KJV)

There is much speculation among translators regarding the exact meaning of the phrase, oftentimes "moving in a mystical direction," as one scholar notes.[20] Some believe the word means a silence or breeze, but others have pointed out that because Elijah audibly heard it, the quietness or stillness was not absolute.[21] Whether we call it a whisper, breeze, or still small voice, God spoke in the simple rather than the grandiose. And in the same way, God calls us to listen in the quiet rather than pout and beg for incredible displays.

How have you experienced God speaking to you in a "gentle whisper"? List any specific memories or situations that come to mind:

God didn't comment on Elijah's reasons for his discouragement, including the idolatry of his fellow Israelites or his aloneness. Instead, He told him to come out and meet Him. One commentator notes that "all these physical phenomena were known to be often precursors of God's coming," such as we see in passages such as Exodus 19:16-18; Judges 5:4-5; and 2 Samuel 22:8-16.[22] God's response reminds me of Job's conversations with God. Job begged for his questions to be answered, but instead God reminded Job of His character. We won't always understand the reasons behind God's decisions or allowances. He calls us to trust Him in the meantime and listen for His voice in the quiet. God can do amazingly and abundantly more than we could ever ask or think (Ephesians 3:20), but He doesn't always operate in the realm of the spectacular.

God calls us to listen in the quiet rather than pout and beg for incredible displays.

Francis Chan challenged high school students to be willing to serve God in the ordinary as well as the spectacular. How about you? Are you longing to be part of something amazing and spectacular for God? You may not want a huge display from God but would love to hear God's still small voice of comfort, direction, or encouragement. If so, how can you first be obedient in the small things God has asked of you? Will you pray, serve, study, and rest according to His leading? Let's spend some time right now listening for the still small voice of the Holy Spirit in our lives.

Talk with God

Because times of quiet are so rare in my life, I'm betting they might be an issue for you as well. Between the notifications on our phones, the conversations with the people in our lives, and the demands of work, family, and ministry, we don't have a lot of margin for quiet. So I have purposely made this a shorter lesson so that you may have some dedicated moments for stillness. Would you set a timer on your phone, tablet, or watch and take the next five to ten minutes to sit and listen?

- Ask God any questions you may have.
- Listen for any questions God may have for you.
- Reread 1 Kings 19:11-13 several times.
- Meditate on the verse you chose on Day 1 as a promise to claim in prayer (page 87).
- Write any insights, encouragement, conviction, or instructions you hear from God in the margin, or write them in a notebook or journal.

DAY 5: THE TOILET BOWL

Today's Scripture Focus

1 Kings 19:13-18

Have you ever had one thought that spiraled into another and then another and, before you knew it, a story of doom and gloom had been written in your mind? My friend refers to this as the "toilet bowl effect."

A teen girl texted me today in a panic. She said that a counselor she met with mentioned that she had a "flat affect." The counselor told her this to help her understand that her emotions were not always evident by her facial expressions and body language. Knowing this could help her understand some communication breakdown with her parents. At times they thought she was apathetic toward things when she really did care. She just had a more stoic response because of the way God wired her.

This sweet teen gal decided to Google "flat affect," and from what she read, she thought she might have borderline personality disorder. Over the next twenty minutes she had diagnosed herself as possibly having schizophrenia and depression as well. I talked her down through our texts, trying to help her understand that having a more stoic personality doesn't mean she has all these things going on. The toilet bowl effect was spinning her thoughts into a downward spiral.

Okay, time to fess up. Have you ever Googled something and started creating a story or diagnosis in your mind? Maybe you haven't, but can you relate to your thoughts spinning out of control from time to time?

I know I can. These are the times we especially need others in the body of Christ to help us realign with the truths we know. Long periods of isolation can be a breeding ground for spiraling thoughts, so we must constantly realign ourselves with God's Word and His people. Elijah had been struggling with toilet bowl thinking throughout 1 Kings 19. After God revealed Himself to Elijah in a whisper, God repeated the same question to Elijah.

According to 1 Kings 19:13, what was God's question?

When you compare Elijah's reply in 1 Kings 19:14 to 1 Kings 19:10, what do you notice?

Elijah gave the exact same answer that he had provided the first time God asked the question. Seeing the whirlwind, fire, and earthquake and then hearing the still small voice hadn't changed his answer. He still felt alone. He thought no other prophets of Yahweh existed. God asked him what he was doing, and he basically said he had given up on His ministry. He felt the Israelites were beyond hope. They had killed the prophets, and he was all alone.

While we may not feel like the rest of the world is worshiping counterfeits, many of us have felt on the outside of friendship circles, family groups, church groups, or coworker clusters. Other times we've watched the news or suffering going on around us and questioned if what we do for God's kingdom really matters. Toilet bowl thinking can lead to a place of despair unless we continually realign ourselves with God's grace and hope.

While some commentators see God's question to Elijah as a rebuke, others point out that it seems more of an invitation. God wanted Elijah to be at a

We aren't always ready to hear God's specific instructions until He lovingly prepares us as only He can.

place where he could hear the truth. Yahweh provided Elijah with soul care under a broom tree and a journey of forty days in the wilderness to give time for processing all that happened on the mountaintop of Carmel; then He spoke in a whisper. God had prepared Elijah to hear the next instructions from a place of understanding.

As Elijah walked through this maze, he may not have been able to see God's preparation and grace. There have been many times when I have seen things in retrospect that I couldn't have understood in the moment. Before I heard God's call to write Bible studies, I went through a weary season in my life when I had a lot of questions and sensed God had some questions for me. After doing some evaluation, praying, fasting, and weathering some storms, I heard God in the quiet. His call was scary but clear. Looking back I can trace His hand in preparing me.

As you reflect on the seasons in your life, can you think of a specific way you can see God's hand in retrospect that you couldn't identify in the moment? If so, write a few details about that time below:

God uses different types of circumstances, time lines, and people to break our downward spirals of self-pity. We aren't always ready to hear God's specific instructions until He lovingly prepares us as only He can. Yahweh helped Elijah see that he still had kingdom work to do.

Read 1 Kings 19:15-18, and complete the instructions God gave Elijah as you read them:

Go back the same way you _____.

Travel to the wilderness of _____.

Anoint Hazeael to be king of _____.

Anoint Jehu to be king of _____.

Anoint Elisha to replace you as my _____.

As you review these instructions, does anything stand out to you?

One of the gals in the pilot study noticed that Elisha would be called to be a warrior prophet much like Elijah had been. They both delivered God's Word but also got involved in battle. The fact that God told Elijah to go back the same way he came really resonated with me. Elijah was ready to give up, but God wanted him to go back to the very same people that he was exasperated with. I can think of times when I've been frustrated with people, and the Lord has lovingly listened as I scribbled out all my whining in a journal. As a pastor's wife, daughter-in-law, and friend, I've had my share of weary moments in relationships. God listens and loves when we experience brokenness. Sometimes God moves us in new directions, but often He tells us to go back and stay the course. He sends us right back into the same group of people with fresh vision and purpose.

Can you think of a time when you wanted to quit but, after reflection and prayer, God's instructions were to "go back the same way you came"? If something comes to mind, write about that season in your life below:

How did God encourage you as you went back to an old situation with a new attitude?

Many times we overcomplicate things, and the Lord calls us back to the basics. When I read books and attend conferences, I usually come away challenged not with new information but fresh inspiration to live out the basic truths I know. God did the same in Elijah's life by reminding him of the ministry he had yet to accomplish. He encouraged Elijah by reminding him of his purpose and his people.

Purpose

God encouraged Elijah with the purposes of a prophet. God's instructions involved anointing leaders, which was the role of a prophet. Samuel anointed

> Sometimes God moves us in new directions, but often He tells us to go back and stay the course.

King David (1 Samuel 16:12-13), and Nathan anointed King Solomon (1 Kings 1:34). God called Elijah back to fulfill the role he previously had been given. He had predicted a drought and called down fire, but he also needed to anoint chosen leaders according to the Lord's instructions.

These were not necessarily great men of God, but they were the ones God would use to carry out His justice. In God's instructions for Elijah, we see that He had three areas of leadership in mind:

- International politics—Hazeael
- National politics—Jehu
- Spiritual prophetic work—Elisha

God told Elijah that all hope wasn't lost, reminding him that God's sovereign plan was much bigger than his momentary discouragement. One of the ways God encourages us includes giving us purpose and productivity. Whether it's being a mom, grandmother, teacher, mentor, friend, prayer partner, or another of the creative ways we can live out God's mission, having a purpose can be a great source of encouragement.

What is one specific thing God has called you to do that gives you purpose?

Are there some ways you sense God calling you to lean into your purpose with greater obedience or clarity? List anything that comes to mind:

God has given each of His children a spiritual gift and a way to use it for His glory.

If you are struggling with God's specific calling and purpose in your life right now, know that you are not alone. Elijah certainly went through a season when things weren't clear. If that's you, take heart and keep seeking and listening. Let these words of Jesus encourage you today: "For everyone who asks, receives. Everyone who seeks, finds. And to everyone who knocks, the door will be opened" (Matthew 7:8). Stay the course, believing that God has given each of His children a spiritual gift and a way to use it for His glory.

People

Another way God encouraged Elijah was to correct his wrong assumption that he was alone.

Reread 1 Kings 19:18 and write below how many others had not bowed to Baal:

_____

This was not a small number! God had thousands of followers who had not bought into the counterfeits of their culture. Even when we feel that we are the only one, we are not alone.

In what way do you feel alone right now? Check any that apply, or write your own response:

_____ **a complicated marriage or other relationship**

_____ **grief over someone I've lost**

_____ **a difficult work situation**

_____ **aging parents**

_____ **sleepless nights or weary days with young children**

_____ **challenges with teens or young adult children**

_____ **financial strain**

_____ **a lack of understanding of my current purpose**

_____ **other:_____**

Whatever you may have checked, you are not alone! Increased vulnerability in small groups, social media, and friendships helps us realize that many others face similar situations to ours. While their situations will never be exactly the same as ours, we can find strength through connecting with others who share common ground. Facebook support groups, small-group Bible studies, and local connections can be a huge asset to us so that we do not spiral into the toilet bowl of "no one else could possibly understand what I'm going through!"

Elijah wasn't the only follower of Yahweh left on the planet, but he sure felt like he was the only prophet. He essentially told God twice in 1 Kings 19 that in terms of prophets, "I am the only one left, and now they are trying to kill me, too." (v.10) God wanted him to go back the way he had come and find like-minded people.

When my daughter was first diagnosed with alopecia, I was anxious to connect with other moms whose daughters had walked our path. It wasn't that they had earth-shattering information, but the understanding and connection was invaluable. Other times I have found connecting with other writers, pastors' wives, or mothers of multiples a great encouragement during certain seasons of life.

What are some ways God has encouraged you through connections with those who are like-minded or in similar circumstances?

Is there a step you need to take to connect with others who might have walked a similar journey?

We often need an attitude adjustment so that God can remind us of the big picture.

Purpose and people are two of the ways God called Elijah out of his broken-ness. God graciously reminded Elijah that He had a plan. Just as Elijah needed God's encouragement to get out of his downward spiral of despair, we often need an attitude adjustment so that God can remind us of the big picture. His grace and hope remain alive in the midst of our broken seasons. Even when it seems like the whole world is chasing after counterfeits, He reserves a remnant of followers.

As you reflect on God's instructions to Elijah, where might God be calling *you* to go back? Is there a place where you sense the Holy Spirit leading you to have renewed energy and vision for a mission He has called you to? Maybe it will include new instructions or networks of people, but it means going back to the original call. Write anything that comes to mind as you reflect and pray:

Now come back to the verse you identified on Day 1 (page 87) and have meditated on each day this week. Try to write it from memory if you are able:

When your thoughts start to spiral downward and you feel alone or apathetic, take some time to review this verse. You may want to make it your background picture on your phone or tablet or write it somewhere you will frequently see it.

God longs to share with us His purposes and people. Sometimes He has to bring us on a multifaceted journey in order to help us get to a place where we can see clearly. End today by asking God to give you eyes to see and ears to hear His encouragements.

Talk with God

Thank God for at least one like-minded person that He has put in your life. Then ask Him to show you any ways that you can lean into His calling on your life more fully so that you can experience the joy of being His hands and feet to serve.

Weekly Wrap-Up

Take a moment to review what we've studied this week. Flip back through the lessons and write below an insight from each day that you would like to apply in your life. (Feel free to summarize in your own words or copy an excerpt.)

Day 1: Expectant Prayer

_____

_____

Day 2: I've Had Enough

_____

_____

Day 3: Under the Broom Tree

_____

_____

Day 4: In the Whisper

_____

_____

Day 5: The Toilet Bowl

_____

_____

VIDEO VIEWER GUIDE: WEEK 3

We can be honest with God when we feel _____ and _____.

1 Kings 19:3-4—Elijah flees

Psalm 103:13-14—The Lord is like a compassionate father

Sometimes we need proper _____ and _____ before we can even process our thoughts and our feelings.

1 Kings 19:5-9—God ministers to Elijah under the broom tree

The God who controls nature often speaks to us in a _____ _____voice, so we must _____ intently.

1 Kings 19:9-12—The Lord speaks to Elijah in the quiet

Soul care includes discovering the _____ _____that God has called us to accomplish.

1 Kings 19:1—The Lord gives Elijah instructions

Week 4

Surrender

1 Kings 19:19–22:9

Memory Verse

Accept the way God does things, for who can straighten what he has made crooked?

(Ecclesiastes 7:13)

DAY 1: CLARITY

Weekly Reading Plan

Read 2 Kings 1-8.

Today's Scripture Focus

1 Kings 19:19-21

When I think of people who have physical stamina, athletes come to mind. Swimmers, runners, basketball players, and other athletes endure grueling workouts to gain the mental and physical ability to endure in competition. Great athletes must develop some of the same qualities of spiritual stamina that we have observed in Elijah's life, striving for excellence when it comes to

- **prayer** — asking in faith and believing victory is possible,
- **choices** — recognizing that small and big choices greatly affect outcomes, and
- **soul care** — realizing that seasons of rest and personal care are necessary to go the distance.

This week as we progress beyond the halfway mark in our study, we will add to these key words *surrender*. In order to persevere in the changing seasons of life, we must release to God the things we cannot understand. Initially the name of this chapter was "acceptance." Something about the word just wasn't sitting right with me. As I processed it with my friend and editor, Sally, she helped me realize that we can accept difficult or confusing things about our lives but still hold on to them. "Surrender" goes a step further than "acceptance," releasing to God.

Injustice lurks all around us. The people in Elijah's day faced the need to reconcile the character of God with the harsh realities of life just as we do.

This week Elijah will duck in and out of the scenes at the end of 1 Kings, and we'll see that God had other prophets and servants who also proclaimed Elijah's message that "Yahweh is God." We'll also meet Elijah's apprentice, Elisha, whose name means "Yahweh saves," adding to God's message to His people.[1]

God was working out a sovereign plan behind the scenes of politics, religious counterfeits, and economic plight in the nation of Israel. The people struggled to see beyond their immediate problems to recognize the bigger picture of God's call to relationship. Yet God relentlessly pursued His wayward people, calling them to accept His Word and surrender to His way even in the midst of apparent injustices. In order to develop and maintain spiritual stamina, we must learn to respond to God's grace in the moment even when the harsh realities of life do not make sense to us. This is the surrendered life.

We will find many facets of life yielded to God this week. Today we begin this focus by considering our natural desire for clarity. Before we can accept God's way, we want to understand what He is doing and how He is calling us to take part in His mission—what it is that we are supposed to do. As we find Elijah acting on God's command to begin mentoring his replacement, we will consider how God uses mentoring relationships to provide guidance and purpose and how this requires clarity regarding the choices we make. To set the stage, let's pick up where we left off last week in 1 Kings 19.

Read 1 Kings 19:19-21, and answer the following questions:

What was Elisha doing when Elijah found him? (v. 19)

How many teams of oxen were in the field? (v. 19)

What did Elijah do with his cloak? (v. 19)

When Elisha ran after Elijah, what did he request? (v. 20)

What was Elijah's reply? (v. 20)

What did Elisha do with his oxen and plow? (v. 21)

What was Elisha's new role in regard to Elijah? (v. 21)

Elisha was plowing in the fields with many other teams of workers. In a marked moment, Elijah came and called him out of his day job into full-time ministry. God had instructed Elijah to anoint two kings and to begin the process of mentoring his replacement. And in Elijah and Elisha's encounter, we find several important principles.

1. God uses mentoring relationships to provide clarity and guidance regarding our purpose.

Throughout Scripture we find a biblical pattern of mentoring. Moses trained Joshua to eventually take the reins of leadership for the people of Israel. Elizabeth spoke into Mary's life and inspired her faith when Mary found herself pregnant by the Holy Spirit. Paul took young Timothy under his wing and trained him in ministry. We all need people we can look up to as spiritual examples. I have found my own mentor to be a great help to me in developing spiritual stamina.

As a young mom, I met a woman named Deb. At first I was intimidated by her. She was authentic but also confident. I was drawn to her walk with God and her generosity, friendliness, and ability to admit imperfections. For the past nineteen years, I have watched how Deb lives her life. I call her when I need prayer or encouragement. I ask for advice when I don't know what to do. She isn't perfect, but I joke that she is who I want to be when I grow up. We have cried and laughed together as she has helped me through some very dark times and celebrated with me through many victories.

Do you have a person of faith whom you have looked to for wisdom? If so, what are some practical ways this person has encouraged you spiritually?

Mentors can help guide us as we walk with God in a broken world. Elijah turned Elisha's world upside down by throwing his cloak on him. This was clearly a sign that others understood as a call into full-time ministry. Elijah then provided guidance when Elisha ran after him to ask if he could go back and kiss his parents goodbye.

The desire to say goodbye to family members before answering God's call reminds me of a situation in the New Testament. In Luke 9, Jesus called a disciple to come and follow him.

Read Luke 9:59-62. What did Jesus say to those who wanted to return home before following Him?

Though Jesus emphasized the need for focus and clarity of mission, Elisha's situation was different. In these two stories we find contrasts in what seem like similar situations. Elijah provided guidance to Elisha, reminding him to think about what God was calling him to do. The men in the Luke passage knew what they were to do but had a divided mind-set. One commentator said it this way, "In Luke 9 saying goodbye is an obstacle to kingdom commitment, whereas in 1 Kings 19 it functions as an entry into kingdom service. Elisha goes back to sever his connections, not to delay his commitment."[3]

> **Mentors can help guide us as we walk with God in a broken world.**

Extra Insight

Many commentators suggest that Elisha was likely from an affluent family, pointing out that twelve teams or yoke of oxen meant it was a large farm that could afford so many people working together.[2]

Mentors gain a sense of comradery and purpose as they sow seeds in the lives of others.

Mentors provide guidance as we seek clarity in how to love God and people, and mentees are not the only ones who benefit in this relationship. Mentors also gain a sense of comradery and purpose as they sow seeds in the lives of others. As we saw last week, when Elijah felt alone, God instructed him to go back the way he came and find others who still worshiped Yahweh; then the Lord gave Elijah specific instructions to begin training Elisha. Elijah benefited from this mentoring relationship just as Elisha did.

How do you think mentoring a younger prophet might have benefited Elijah personally?

In what ways have discipling, training, or investing in the spiritual lives of others impacted your own spiritual life?

"Therefore, go and make disciples of all the nations, baptizing them in the name of the Father and the Son and the Holy Spirit. Teach these new disciples to obey all the commands I have given you. And be sure of this: I am with you always, even to the end of the age."

(Matthew 28:19-20)

While sometimes it can be exhausting to teach and train others, it is what we all are called to do. Read Matthew 28:19-20 in the margin, and write below the action verbs Jesus gave to his disciples:

"_____ and _____ disciples..., _____ing them in the name of the Father and the Son and the Holy Spirit. _____ these new disciples to obey all the commands I have given you."

God gave Elijah a mission and purpose when He spoke to him in a still small voice, and one component of these instructions was to train Elisha. God also has given a common mission to all of us who have chosen to follow Jesus. We are to go, make disciples, baptize, and teach others to obey God's commands. Each of us needs clarity in where, how, and on what timetable we are to fulfill this commission personally; and we must wrestle with God and listen to the voice of His Spirit to know how to apply this command in our lives.

Spend some time right now asking God for clarity in how He is calling *you* to make disciples in your sphere of influence. Don't overthink it. It doesn't have to sound glamorous or formal. We can make disciples in so many ways—as mothers, grandmothers, aunts, friends, and coworkers. We can make disciples as we love the downtrodden, teach Sunday school, mentor teenagers or young moms, or encourage a friend at work. It can be casual or more formal depending on our season of life and calling.

As you listen to God, identify one or two ways God has called or is calling you to make disciples in your current season of life:

At times in my life, God has been very clear in His leading about where I am to serve. Other times I have felt lost, distracted, and unsure of how to live out His mission of telling others about His love. Those are the times when we need spiritual stamina more than ever! No matter where you are today, I pray you are seeking God for clarity in how you can share God's love with others. We don't know whether or not Elisha actually went back and kissed his parents, but we do know that he made a clear decision in saying yes to God.

2. Sometimes we must say a clear no to past things in order to say yes to God's call for the future.

Another principle we see in Elijah and Elisha's encounter is the need to discern how to prioritize our time and attention and what we must let go of in order to pursue God's call. Oxen and plows would have been valuable commodities in an agrarian society, but according to 1 Kings 19:21, Elisha said yes to God's call by slaughtering his oxen and roasting them over a fire built with the wood from his plow, offering the townspeople the meat from the oxen, and then leaving home to serve Elijah as his assistant. Why? These three actions show us that new callings are not always glamorous but require us to do hard things, and that saying no to some things is actually necessary before God can move us where we need to go. By eliminating his oxen and plow, Elisha said a strong no to his career. After making this bold move, he couldn't run back to his old profession when prophet life got hard. He left no open door to run home.

I often want to leave a contingency plan in place just in case bold decisions for God don't work out. There have been times when I've added a new ministry option or venture while continuing to do past things as well—which can work for a while. I was babysitting full-time when I started writing Bible studies, but it became difficult to stay on track with research and writing when I began traveling to speak. Despite the challenges, I was scared to let go of the consistent income that babysitting provided for our family. A point came, however, when it was clear I couldn't keep up both ventures. I needed to make a decision by faith, and so I tearfully informed a family I had come to love that I could no longer care for their children.

A lack of focus is one way we can lose stamina in following God. We add new yeses without letting go of other things with some nos. My husband does a great job of keeping things simple with his wardrobe. When he brings in a new shirt, he gets rid of an old one. He does the same thing with shoes. If he gets a new pair, he throws out an old pair. I, on the other hand, tend to get new things but hang on to old ones—just in case I might need them. This causes my closet to become cluttered and overloaded.

The same thing can happen in life. When we add new callings but still cling to the old, we can lose focus. Sometimes in order to surrender to God's way, we must be willing to let go. Elisha had to let go of his farmer's life. So, he made some bold moves to keep him from being tempted to go back.

Where is God calling *you* to burn the plow in order to move forward? Think about your time commitments, emotional bandwidth, and God's specific call on your life. Is there an area where God is calling you to say a firm no to one thing in order to say yes to something else? Write below anything that comes to mind:

Moving forward in obedience might necessitate leaving behind old habits, letting go of ministry commitments, or even moving to a new city. Such "losses" can be painful but necessary. We can't hold anything too tightly, whether that means people, jobs, ministries, or homes. At times God might ask us to give up our affections, security, or familiarity to follow Him wholeheartedly. The good news is that He will work mightily in the new calling when we are willing to let go at His direction. Elijah mentored Elisha, who eventually replaced him as God's mouthpiece to the people of Israel. God had something important ahead for Elisha, but he had to be willing to loosen his grip on farming in order to move ahead into the life of a prophet.

Our yes-and-no answers are important. When I have said yes to too many ministry opportunities, I later have realized that it meant saying no to family time. We must be discerning about how we spend both our yeses and our nos. We are prone to dabble with many half-commitments, but God calls us to focus. Letting go can be difficult, but clutter keeps us from clarity; so, we must learn the power of no.

3. We all need accountability.

We also find in the story of Elijah and Elisha's encounter the principle of accountability. Elisha shared the meat with the people of the town, letting others know of his commitment. Imagine the buzz of conversation as the community ate the oxen meat. Now that people knew that Elisha was called to become a prophet, they could encourage him and keep him accountable if he tried to quit and run home.

I find that when I tell people about a decision or leading from God, it helps to hold me accountable. At certain times I have felt led to fast from television or wear a bracelet reminding me not to complain. Knowing that I have told others about my commitment helps me stay the course when I am tempted to quit prematurely. Saying something out loud to others brings a new level of surrender as we realize we aren't the only ones who know the specific thing that God has told us to do.

> **Recall your answer to the previous question where you identified a no God is calling you to say to one thing in order to say yes to something else. Identify someone with whom you can share this for accountability:**

4. New callings are not always glamorous.

A final principle in the calling of Elisha is that God's callings are not easy but usually require stamina. After Elisha burned his bridges to his farming career and shared with the townspeople his intent to become a prophet, he then went and served Elijah. He didn't just talk about it and throw a party to celebrate it; he actually did it, and it wasn't an easy assignment.

> **Take another look at 1 Kings 19:21 in the margin. What word is used to describe Elisha's role?**

Elisha was an *assistant* to Elijah—a role similar to that of a servant. Yet it was in this humble position that he would learn from the great prophet Elijah and later receive a double portion of Elijah's spirit (2 Kings 2:9). First Corinthians 4:20 encourages us with these words: "For the Kingdom of God is not just a lot of talk; it is living by God's power." Once we have determined what God is calling us to do, we must follow Elisha's example and put one foot in front of the other in humble obedience. Elisha was committed to God's mission and Elijah's call to apprenticeship. We learn from his example that God's call must determine everything we do, and this requires the heart of a servant.

So Elisha returned to his oxen and slaughtered them. He used the wood from the plow to build a fire to roast their flesh. He passed around the meat to the townspeople, and they all ate. Then he went with Elijah as his assistant.

(1 Kings 19:21)

But Jehoshaphat asked, "Is there no prophet of the LORD here, through whom we may inquire of the LORD?"

An officer of the king of Israel answered, "Elisha son of Shaphat is here. He used to pour water on the hands of Elijah."

(2 Kings 3:11 NIV)

New callings are not always glamorous. In fact, they often require us to roll up our sleeves and serve.

Read 2 Kings 3:11 in the margin. What does this verse tell us that Elisha did?

Elisha was not just a prophet in training but also a personal servant who washed his master's hands. I wonder if there were moments when Elisha was weary of the boring moments of prophet life or questioned God's purpose. Perhaps he longed for the days he had shared with his friends behind the plow. No doubt there were times when Elisha had to recall the marked moment in the field when Elijah had put his cloak over him so that he could continue to trust God's call. When we become discouraged or long for the things we offered up to God when we answered His call, we too must remember past moments of clarity.

After I stopped babysitting to write and speak full time, it wasn't always easy. Although I found myself having more flexibility with my time, I now had to navigate some uncharted waters. There was much to learn about time management, deadlines, marketing, and scheduling. I made a lot of mistakes, but I chose to "fail forward" in pursuit of pleasing God rather than others. God's specific call on your life may look much different than mine, but we both share the common mission to go, make disciples, and teach others to obey; and this likely will include some great moments as well as some frustrating ones. We must accept that God's plan is good even when we do not understand the big picture. By serving, completing simple tasks, and meeting needs, we are exercising our faith until we understand more fully God's ultimate plan.

Both Elijah and Elisha put everything on the line to follow God's call. They were committed to each other and to God. Today Jesus is calling us to follow Him with clarity and focus. We are guaranteed to grow in faith and stamina as we accept His unique assignments to share His love!

Talk with God

Ask the Holy Spirit to reveal any new directions you are to take in regard to mentoring relationships in your life. Listen for any areas where you need to let go with a no in order to move forward with a yes.

New callings are not always glamorous. They often require us to roll up our sleeves and serve.

DAY 2: KNOWING GOD

**Today's
Scripture
Focus**

1 Kings 20

In my Bible study group last week, a gal shared that she was struggling with leaving time and space in her thought life to listen to God. After completing her Bible study homework, she would typically turn on a radio or TV program to occupy her mind. Even though the content that she listened to was good, it became a constant stream of information. She recognized a need to take time to process what she was learning from God's Word by reflecting on it, talking to God about it, and listening to Him.

That same day in a phone conversation, another friend expressed a similar concern about her own life. She said that she was taking in a lot of knowledge of God but not spending much personal time getting to know Him or processing what she was learning. These two friends weren't talking about some one-time experiential moment or emotional expression but an ongoing relationship—knowing God personally rather than knowing about Him. How can we tell the difference? J. I. Packer described it this way: "There's a difference between knowing God and knowing about God. When you truly know God, you have energy to serve Him, boldness to share Him, and contentment in Him."[4] Knowing God results in energy, boldness, and true contentment or peace.

Never before in history have we had access to such a large amount of knowledge about God.

What are some different information avenues that you have utilized to learn more about God?

We can read books, take classes or do Bible studies, listen to sermons or podcasts, and find a wealth of good information through the Internet. Having knowledge of God can be a great way to lead us into deeper relationship with Him. However, it's possible to have an extensive secondhand knowledge of God and the practice of Christianity without having a close relationship with Christ. In our information-affluent world, we can know a lot about the lives of favorite bands, famous actors, or government officials but not actually have a personal relationship with any of them. In the same way, we must be careful not to know a lot of stuff about God, the church, and the Bible without *engaging* in a close relationship with the living Christ.

Today we will find in our study of 1 Kings 20 that God longs to be known. Before we make some connections regarding how we can know God better, let's get some context for what was going on in the kingdom of Israel at this time.

Read 1 Kings 20:1-12 and fill in the speech bubbles below, paraphrasing the words of King Ben-hadad (King B) and King Ahab (King A):

King B (v. 3)

King A (v. 4)

King B (vv. 5-6)

In verses 7-8, the elders of Israel advise King Ahab.

King A (v. 9)

King B (v. 10)

King A (v. 11)

In verse 12, King Ben-hadad's army prepares to attack.

King Ahab was threatened with an attack from the Arameans. King Ben-hadad wasn't content to take the best people and treasures of Israel; he wanted it all. In this exchange between the two kings, we see that Ahab stood up to him yet still faced an imminent attack.

Now that we have some context, read 1 Kings 20:13-22. Write the last sentence of verse 13 below:

Although Ahab didn't ask for Yahweh's help, God sent a prophet with a message of hope to him.

While we do not know where Elijah and Elisha were during this critical time in the Israelites' history, we are reminded that God was not utilizing their obedience alone. We must remember that even when we are not a part of the story, God is still working. We can get so wrapped up in our own worlds that we forget God is revealing Himself to other people, churches, and cultures. God wants everyone to know Him, and He is doing things we may or may not know about.

Ahab and the people of Israel had to decide how they would respond to God's grace in this moment. Though they did not seek Yahweh, Yahweh sought Ahab and spoke to him through a prophet; and Ahab chose to listen to and obey this prophet of God. This brings us to our first key concept for knowing God.

1. To know God, we must respond to His grace.

Ahab was a wicked king, and he likely responded to God's message out of desperation. Even so, he chose to respond. Whether we're desperate or on top of the world, we too choose how we will respond to God's words to us.

In Ahab's day, God's message came through prophets. Today we have the Word of God. Through the Bible we hear God's gospel of grace—that He sent His Son to earth on our behalf so that we could be reconciled to Him and know Him intimately. Just as God called the nation of Israel to know Him through the law and prophets, He calls us to know Him intimately through His Word and His living Word, Jesus.

What are some ways that you can get to know someone?

You may have written some ideas that have to do with communicating or spending time together. Both involve responding. There can be no relationship without a response.

God was gracious to the nation of Israel by showing up, giving a word of promise and a word of warning, and inviting their response. The word of promise was that Ahab would be victorious over Ben-hadad. The word of warning was that Ben-hadad would be back, and the Israelites needed to prepare.

God has given us a word of promise through the gospel. He sent His Son into the world as an act of grace to overcome sin and death and restore us to close relationship with God. We must choose how we will respond to this message of victory. God also gives us a word of warning, essentially calling us to stop trying to live according to our own ability or understanding. Instead, He calls us to know Him.

What are some truths or actions that have helped you move beyond knowing about God to knowing Him personally?

If you had a hard time answering this question, you might do what I did and work in reverse. I noticed that my intimacy with God is adversely affected when I:

- allow my prayer life to become perfunctory or rote;
- choose to rush through Bible reading and study rather than reflect, meditate, and think deeply about God's truths;
- do not get enough sleep, exercise, or healthy food;
- fail to fully surrender to God's way, especially in difficult times;
- withdraw from nourishing Christian community and accountability; and
- serve out of duty or guilt rather than love for God and a desire to be faithful.

So, the opposites of these things are what help me stay close to Jesus. Many of these practices are related to the key concepts for spiritual stamina we are studying in Elijah's life: prayer, choices, soul care, surrender, mentoring, and legacy. To help us draw near to God, we can identify some warning signs that there is distance in our relationship and we need to give it some time and attention. Because every relationship has mountaintop, valley, and plateau seasons, we must *continually* pursue a close relationship with Jesus. Responding to His grace is one way we can do this.

There can be no relationship without a response.

Because every relationship has mountaintop, valley, and plateau seasons, we must *continually* pursue a close relationship with Jesus.

2. To know God, we must remember that He is a powerful God who cares about everything that concerns us.

A second key concept when it comes to knowing God is acknowledging that our all-powerful God is in the details of our lives.

Read 1 Kings 20:23-30, and write the last sentence of verse 28 below:

Why did the Arameans under Ben-hadad's leadership think they lost the last battle against Israel? (v. 23)

God wants us to know that He is not limited.

The Arameans believed that Yahweh was limited. Since Israel was a land of hills, they wrongly assumed He could not help His people in the valleys. God would dispel this myth by giving Israel victory. As with the Israelites and Arameans, God wants us to know that He is not limited. Sometimes we put Him in a box, thinking He is able to act only in a certain way. Have you ever thought things like this?

- This problem is too big for God (e.g., cancer, death, financial crisis).
- This detail is too small for God (e.g., clothes, a cold, car repairs).

Like the Arameans, we can limit God or put Him in a box—whether by thinking He isn't able to help us or isn't concerned about the details of our lives.

In a conversation with my brother about a job opportunity, I once asked him if he had prayed about the situation. He said he didn't think God cared much where he worked, stating that God had bigger concerns such as poverty and war. I shared with Him that Scripture tells us God "delights in every detail of [our] lives" (Psalm 37:23). The Lord cares about our jobs, our relationships, and even the daily minutia. He knows the number of hairs on our heads (Luke 12:7) and longs for us to draw near to Him (James 4:8). We also know that nothing is too difficult for Him (Jeremiah 32:27).

God is not limited in any way. He wants us to communicate with Him in the good times and the bad times. He wants to know about the big things and the little things in our lives.

Spend a few moments telling the Lord about the big things you are facing and the little things you are concerned about that may seem

insignificant in the grand scheme of things. Remember that God delights in the details. Write below anything you hear from God or any verses from Scripture the Holy Spirit brings to mind:

3. To know God, we must accept that He is a God of both grace and judgment.

The last key concept of knowing God from today's passage is remembering that God is both just and gracious. We must accept this truth if we are to know God beyond surface information about Him.

Finish 1 Kings 20 by reading verses 31-43, and write a short summary of what took place:

King Ahab may seem nice and enlightened and tolerant by sparing Benhadad. From our human vantage point, we might even think the king of Israel should be commended for his grace toward the Aramean king. Commenting on this passage, one scholar writes, "We may be tempted to think Ahab is more like Jesus than Yahweh is."[6] Yet in verse 42 we learn that Ahab actually had disobeyed God by sparing the Aramean king.

According to verse 42, what would be the result of King Ahab's disobedience?

As we read Scripture, we must remember that God is both gracious and holy. We cannot always understand His purposes and ways, but we can fully trust Him, knowing that He is just and good.

We learn from this story that if we want to truly know God, then we must respond to His grace, remember that He is not only all-powerful but also concerned about every detail of our lives, and accept that He is both gracious and just.

If we want to have spiritual stamina, we must be clear about God's grace, power, and judgment. And as we develop a deep, consistent relationship with

Christ, we will be able to love and obey Him in every season of life—even if imperfectly.

Talk with God

Pray to the Lord Philippians 3:10-11:

I want to know Christ and experience the mighty power that raised him from the dead. I want to suffer with him, sharing in his death, so that one way or another I will experience the resurrection from the dead!

DAY 3: IT'S NOT FAIR

Today's Scripture Focus

1 Kings 21:1-16, 25

Growing up with three siblings, I have memories of fights over chores, clothes, and privileges, among other things. I often remember saying, "It's not fair"—whether it had to do with a seeming injustice, such as

- my brother having what seemed to be more relaxed rules than we three girls;
- my parents paying for my youngest sister's gas once she got her driver's license, when the rest of us had to pay for it ourselves; and
- my getting stuck doing someone else's chores because she or he wasn't around.

I'll bet you can think of some things you thought were unfair in your childhood too. As we've grown older, the cry of "unfair" hasn't ceased. Injustice seems to be all around us. People who cheat and break rules sometimes seem to get ahead. Children are diagnosed with cancer. Bad things happen to good people. In fact, the older I get, the less "fair" things in this world seem to be. This bothers us so much because we were created in the image of God (Genesis 1:27).

He is the Rock; his deeds are perfect. Everything he does is just and fair. He is a faithful God who does no wrong; how just and upright he is!
(Deuteronomy 32:4)

According to Deuteronomy 32:4 in the margin, what can we know about God's character?

God is just and fair. Because we were created in His image, we have a strong sense of justice. When we encounter rules, circumstances, or situations that seem unfair, we have a variety of reactions. We might get angry, bitter, or just plain confused.

What are some unfair things you have noticed lately?

Whether you listed a personal situation, a natural disaster, or a global problem, injustice of any kind does not sit well with us. We need spiritual stamina to continue trusting in God's justice when life does not make sense. Today we will explore three important truths related to God's justice. To set the stage for this exploration, let's dive into 1 Kings 21.

Read 1 Kings 21:1-14, and answer the following questions:

What did Ahab want and why? (v. 2)

What was Naboth's reply? (v. 3)

How did Ahab respond to Naboth's reply? (v. 4)

How did Jezebel react when Ahab told her the situation? (v. 7)

Briefly explain what Jezebel did to manipulate circumstances to get the vineyard? (vv. 8-14)

Ahab wanted Naboth's vineyard to use as a vegetable garden because it was near his property. His offer seemed fair in that he said he would exchange it for a different vineyard or pay Naboth for it. However, Naboth refused.

What can we learn about God's justice from this story?

1. We should ask God rather than manipulate people and situations to get what we want.

Ahab's reaction was that of a spoiled child. He basically cried, "It's not fair," throwing a tantrum that included being angry and sullen, going to bed with his face to the wall, and refusing to eat.

Sometimes when we don't get what we want, we can throw our own fits. None of us gets our way all the time. We can't buy everything we want. Others are promoted when we feel more qualified. We prefer traditional music but they keep playing that loud stuff at church. You get the gist.

What childlike behaviors have you witnessed when others did not get what they wanted?

Some of the gals who piloted this study mentioned social media rants, passive-aggressive behavior, pettiness, purposely leaving someone out, and gossip. We may not go to bed and refuse to eat, but we can get angry and pout like Ahab when things don't go the way we planned.

According to James 4:2 in the margin, what should we do when we want something?

You want what you don't have, so you scheme and kill to get it. You are jealous of what others have, but you can't get it, so you fight and wage war to take it away from them. Yet you don't have what you want because you don't ask God for it.

(James 4:2)

James 4:2 could have been written just for Ahab and Jezebel! Ahab didn't pray or seek counsel from God. Instead, he whined until his wife took drastic measures, manipulating and scheming.

What strikes me about Jezebel's plan is that she used a religious gathering, which was centered around a fast, as the setting for meeting the legal requirement of obtaining two witnesses when making accusations.

The false charge against Naboth was that he had cursed God and the king. In Naboth's case, politicians used lies, murder, and cheating to bring about the charge of cursing God. And tragically, this farce of an accusation ended in Naboth's wrongful death. We learn from Ahab's wrong reaction that we should bring our desires to God rather than scheme to get what we want.

2. God calls us to stand up against injustice.

This tragedy of Naboth's death might have been prevented if any number of people would have stood up to Jezebel. The elders and town leaders could have stood up for justice. The two scoundrels could have refused to lie. Ahab could have told Jezebel she was going too far. But no one was will willing to take a stand.

Read 1 Kings 21:15-16. What did Ahab do when Jezebel gave him the news of Naboth's death?

Jezebel was a scary woman. I'm sure it wouldn't have been easy to stand up to her. The elders and town leaders probably felt they had to go along with her plan. There likely have been times in our own lives when we've felt powerless to stand up against something we knew wasn't right.

Has there been a time when you felt powerless to stand up against injustice? If so, describe it briefly:

Read Proverbs 31:8-9 in the margin. What are we called to do?

Although we cannot fight every battle, we are called to speak up for those who can't speak for themselves and work for justice for those who are oppressed.

The heroes of the past are often those who stood up to injustice. Corrie ten Boom hid Jews during World War II. She became involved personally when others turned a blind eye to the injustices around them. Amy Carmichael was a missionary to India who helped rescue children from temple prostitution. Getting involved cost them both greatly. Corrie ten Boom spent years in a concentration camp, and Amy Carmichael faced kidnapping charges and death threats. Both took risks to speak up for those who were poor and helpless. Though we live in a different time than these two women, we still have many opportunities to take risks and make sacrifices to ensure justice for those around us.

What are some tangible ways you have seen others get personally involved in speaking up or ensuring justice for others?

> **Although we cannot fight every battle, we are called to speak up for those who can't speak for themselves.**

> *Speak up for those who cannot speak for themselves;*
> *ensure justice for those being crushed.*
> *Yes, speak up for the poor and helpless,*
> *and see that they get justice.*
> *(Proverbs 31:8-9)*

Are there ways that you also have joined the fight—in the past or more recently?

Many of my friends have helped children in need through foster care and adoption. Sponsoring children in third world countries by partnering with trustworthy organizations that provide food, basic healthcare, and education is a practical way to help those who are poor and powerless. We also can stand against injustice by fighting for freedom and human rights in many other ways, including writing, speaking, giving, serving, and raising awareness or advocating for the rights of others.

Take a moment to write a prayer below, asking God where He might be calling you to get involved in someone's life at this time:

Life definitely isn't fair. Some people are born with physical or mental limitations while others are not. Many children around the globe do not have access to clean water, medicine, or nurturing families. We will find as the story plays out in Scripture that God did pronounce indictments against Ahab and Jezebel, but not before Naboth was dragged outside of town and stoned to death. In my humanness, I wonder why God didn't intervene before Naboth suffered and died. It doesn't seem fair.

I tend to want God to right all the wrongs in a way that makes sense to me. Do you ever feel this way at times? My friend Marybeth calls it cognitive dissonance. I know God is good and all-powerful, yet bad stuff happens all the time. I don't understand why Naboth died and Ahab lived. It doesn't make sense that a three-year-old boy in my church has a brain tumor. I don't understand why my dear friend is going through a brutal divorce. It is difficult to reconcile the injustices we encounter, but we can either choose to despair or trust that one day God will right every wrong (as we will explore next). And in the meantime, we can be the hands and feet of God in this world, bringing His kingdom here on earth, as we stand against injustice.

3. Ultimately, we can entrust justice into God's hands.

Because our God is good and just, we must continually surrender our cognitive dissonance to Him.

Read 1 Kings 21:17-26, and label the following statements T (true) or F (false):

_____ 1. God's message to Ahab was, "Wasn't it enough that you killed Naboth? Must you rob him, too?"

_____ 2. God said cats would lick Ahab's blood at the very place where they licked the blood of Naboth.

_____ 3. Ahab exclaimed that Elijah was his friend.

_____ 4. Elijah told Ahab that God would destroy all of his male descendants.

_____ 5. Jezebel's body would be eaten by dogs at the plot of land in Jezreel.

_____ 6. Members of Ahab's family who died in the city would be eaten by vultures and those who died in the fields would be eaten by dogs.

_____ 7. Ahab had sold himself to what was evil in the Lord's sight under the influence of his wife, Jezebel, and his worst outrage was worshiping idols.

God saw what Jezebel and Ahab had done to Naboth, and he sent Elijah to tell Ahab about the reckoning that was coming for his actions. God said that He would deal with Ahab and Jezebel.

God promises to punish the wicked. He is just. While His justice sometimes may seem to us to be late or even nonexistent, we must trust God's character. As one commentator put it, "We mustn't allow our quandary over the timing of Yahweh's justice to eclipse our comfort over the fact of it."[7] When I'm struggling over a particular injustice, I rehearse the truths I know about God's justice and surrender those things beyond my control into God's loving hands, believing that ultimately He will sort out rewards and punishments.

Draw a star beside the following verse that resonates most strongly with you today when it comes to God's justice:

For the LORD loves justice,
and he will never abandon the godly.
(Psalm 37:28a)

Answers: 1.T 2.F 3.F 4.T 5.T 6.F 7.T

Evil people will surely be punished,
  but the children of the godly will go free.
          (Proverbs 11:21)

Dear friends, never take revenge. Leave that to the righteous anger of God. For the Scriptures say,

  "I will take revenge;
  I will pay them back,"
  says the LORD.

          (Romans 12:19)

Life doesn't always make sense, but we can find peace when we wait, trust, and rest in God's grace and judgment. Only He has the right and the ability to carry out perfect justice that is both unbiased and merciful.

Talk with God

Tell God about your confusion when it comes to His timing, inaction, or anything else that has left you confused or sad lately. Ask God to help you grow in faith as you build stamina to believe His Word even when your circumstances do not seem to line up with it. Pray for wisdom to know when and how to stand up against injustice.

DAY 4: THE POWER OF HUMILITY

Today's Scripture Focus

1 Kings 21:27-29

My pride can flare in the worst way when my husband and I get into disagreements. Even when I know I am wrong, I sometimes make excuses, justify myself, and put up walls of silence with a prideful, self-righteous attitude. My first reaction is usually not to admit my faults, mourn over them, and seek forgiveness. The Holy Spirit helps me on a path to humility, but it takes time and inner wrestling to get to that posture.

Whether it is in your work, ministry, or family relationships, can you relate to the battle with pride when you've done something wrong? Briefly explain your response.

This week we've been learning about the power of surrender when it comes to spiritual stamina. So far this week we've studied (1) how Elisha surrendered to God's call into ministry, saying no to farming in order to say yes to serving Elijah; (2) how God's people surrendered to His gracious intervention in helping them win a war against the Aramean king Ben-hadad; and (3) how difficult it can be to surrender when it comes to injustices like Naboth experienced at the hands of King Ahab and Queen Jezebel. Today we will find some verses that remind us of a powerful weapon when it comes to surrender.

Read 1 Kings 21:27-29. What did Ahab do that God responded to with mercy?

He _____ himself before God

Yesterday we read that Ahab pouted and threw a fit about a vineyard he couldn't have. So Jezebel planned to have the owner Naboth killed. After Naboth's death, Ahab went right away to claim the land he desired. God saw these wicked actions and sent Elijah to tell Ahab some pretty scary things that would happen as a result of his bad choices. Then Ahab did something out of character by humbling himself.

According to verse 27, what were some specific things that Ahab did to humble himself?

Ahab tore his clothes, wore burlap, fasted, and mourned. Then God softened the blow on His pronouncements against Ahab. God didn't fully take away the consequences, but He did say that Ahab would not be alive to witness the horror to come. These verses stand out in contrast to the firm hand God had displayed against King Ahab in the past. Here we see the incredible compassion of our God—even toward those we might consider the worst of sinners.

As you reflect on Ahab's life and God's willingness to amend Ahab's punishment based on his humility, do any questions arise in your heart and mind? If so, note them below:

Extra Insight

Some examples of delayed punishment after someone has demonstrated repentance include Hezekiah (2 Kings 20:1, 6, 11) and Nineveh (Jonah 3:10).[8]

Here are some things that come to my mind:

- When King Ben-hadad of Aramea (Syria) asked for grace and Ahab spared him, God responded with punishment. How are we to know when to extend grace and when to follow through with consequences?
- According to this chapter, God said something would happen to Ahab, but then He did not follow through when Ahab showed humility. Did God change His mind?

Have you ever wondered about such things? Let's consider each question.

First, there's the question of God's grace. We find throughout Scripture that God always responds to humility with grace. Jesus upheld the law with the proud but showed grace to the humble. Because God knows every heart, He knows whether someone is truly humble and repentant.

When Ahab showed Ben-hadad mercy and got into trouble for it, we can assume he had not sought God's guidance and wisdom because Scripture says that his pardon was an act of direct disobedience to God's instructions. There also is no mention of Ben-hadad ever repenting with mourning and fasting. Instead, He had come back to attack God's people once again.

Have you ever seen lack of consequences lead to entitlement or pride in the lives of others? If so, how?

God calls parents, leaders, and others in authority to lovingly discipline. By this I mean following the guidance of the Holy Spirit in giving or allowing consequences in the lives of those God has placed under our care. If a prideful child never receives consequences and continues on a destructive path, it isn't very loving to keep shielding that child from the pain of his or her choices. The writer of Proverbs said this: "Those who love their children care enough to discipline them" (13:24b). In the same way, we know that God disciplines those He loves (Hebrews 12:6). Both removing and enforcing consequences can be loving acts when they are led by God. We must listen to the leading of the Holy Spirit to know which course of action is truly best for those God has placed under our care.

How do you discern when to make allowances for the faults of others and when to implement boundaries or consequences?

One principle we find in God's response to Ahab here in 1 Kings 21 is that humility brings out the gracious nature of our God. It often is the same with us.

One night one of my teenage daughters broke several family rules, including not letting me know where she was, and I was scared about her whereabouts. I could not reach her, and I was freaking out, as my kids say. So I left our small group Bible study to go look for her, and a friend graciously came along to drive me. When we got to my house and found my daughter in the living room, away from the phone I had been calling for over an hour, I reprimanded her and cried simultaneously. (I didn't even know that was possible.)

As we all got back into the car to take my daughter to her own Bible study group, she started to explain herself and make excuses. I told her that it would be better to simply own her mistakes. At that point she got quiet, giving us both time and space to think. Later when she got home, she told me she was so sorry, she knew she had done wrong, and she hadn't meant to scare me. When she humbly owned her mistakes, something within me shifted.

Have you ever been angry at someone only to have that feeling melt away as the person expresses grief over the pain he or she has caused? If an example comes to mind, record it below:

Because of the power of humility, I want to learn to get to a humble attitude more quickly as my daughter did. It is our battle with pride that keeps us from it. C. S. Lewis wrote this about pride:

> According to Christian teachers, the essential vice, the utmost evil, is Pride.... Pride leads to every other vice: it is the complete anti-God state of mind...it is Pride which has been the chief cause of misery in every nation and every family since the world began.[9]

According to C. S. Lewis, pride leads to every other vice. So, let's consider a few verses that address pride and humility.

Read the following passages, writing below words related to pride and words related to humility:

Scripture	Pride	Humility
Proverbs 11:2		
Micah 6:8		
Ephesians 4:2		
James 4:6-10		

How would you summarize God's message about pride in these passages?

One thing we can always count on is God's commitment to grace and mercy.

As we read the breadth of Scripture, we begin to understand why the mourning, fasting, and repentance of Ahab had such an effect on our loving Father. You might say that humility gets Him every time! But as we will come to find, Ahab's repentance was short-lived; and God knew it would be. One commentator said this: "Who is a God like Yahweh with such gusto for mercy?"[10]

Our God has gusto for mercy! This gives us stamina when life is complicated and unclear. One thing we can always count on is God's commitment to grace and mercy.

Now let's briefly consider my second question regarding God's response to Ahab's change of heart. God says in Malachi 3:6a, "I am the LORD, and I do not change," and in Hosea 11:8, "My heart is changed within me; all my compassion is aroused" (NIV). These verses seem to contradict themselves until we understand that God is actually acting according to His very nature whenever He responds with compassion, grace, and mercy to those who are humble. God tells us again and again in Scripture that He values humility. He promises that when we humble ourselves, He will act—He will lift us up (James 4:10). He isn't changing His mind about sin; instead, He is being true to His character by being responsive to a sincere, humble heart.

Throughout our study this week we've had a front-row seat to the life of Ahab, the most wicked king of Israel. As we've read previously, "No one else so completely sold himself to what was evil in the LORD's sight as Ahab did under the influence of his wife Jezebel" (1 Kings 21:25). If God could see the humility of Ahab and relent, then those of us living on this side of the cross have an even a greater hope! Jesus paid the price for all our sins! The key is to humble ourselves before God and receive His forgiveness, thanking Jesus for paying the price so that we could be forgiven and made righteous.

Ahab's humility included wearing burlap, fasting, and mourning. I don't know about you, but I don't have any burlap at my house to sleep in if I want to show God sorrow over my sin. And in light of Jesus' work on the cross, He is more interested in a heart change rather than any outward expression.

In light of what Jesus has done for us, what are some ways we can show humility before God?

Take some time to reflect, asking God to reveal any areas where He is calling you to humble yourself. Write a short action step next to anything that applies:

In your marriage

At work

In your church

With your immediate and/or extended family

Toward a difficult person in your life

On social media

Other:

Pride is dangerous. The one glimmer of hope in Ahab's lifelong string of prideful statements and behaviors is these few verses tucked away in 1 Kings 21. If there is hope for Ahab through humility, there is even more hope for us who put our faith and trust in Jesus our Savior. None of us is beyond the reach of repentance. As Anglican priest and author John Stott said, "Pride is your greatest enemy, humility is your greatest friend."[11] I want to make humility my greatest friend. I hope you do too. Humility will give us the spiritual stamina we need to keep on loving God and pursuing Him in every season of our lives.

Talk with God

Many of the Scriptures about humility that we read today relate to prayer. In your prayer time, make humility the centerpiece of your dialogue with God. Confess sin, taking responsibility for what you've done wrong, and thank Him for his grace and forgiveness. If you like, end your time with these lines from the serenity prayer:

God grant me the serenity to accept the things I cannot change; courage to change the things I can; and wisdom to know the difference.[12]

DAY 5: CAREFUL SURRENDER

Today's Scripture Focus

1 Kings 22

During my college years, I spent one summer in Japan teaching English. My favorite part of each week was a team meeting when four other college students who taught in neighboring cities would gather together. We ate fast food, spoke fast English, and supported one another as we celebrated good experiences and brainstormed together the challenges we faced. I had to take a bus and then a train to get to the town where we met. After everyone was at the train station, we shared a taxi to our destination, which was a nearby church. One week my bus didn't come on time, and I had to catch a later train. By the time I arrived at the train station, my team had already left in a taxi. When I called the church from the station, we decided it would be too expensive for me to take my own taxi. So, the person at the church told me which bus to take and gave me the name of the stop I should listen for so that I would know when to get off.

I thought I followed the directions, but I never heard my stop called. After about forty-five minutes of riding and watching everyone else get off, I watched as the bus pulled into the terminal and the driver looked at me. I tried to communicate, but he spoke very little English; and my Japanese was worse than his English. The word *lost* took on new meaning for me in that moment! The kind driver took me inside, and we called my contact person. After the driver spoke with him in Japanese, we got back on the bus; and I received a personal ride to my correct destination, which took about an hour. The driver would not let me pay him a cent.

I accepted the advice about which bus to take, but clearly I did not apply that advice accurately!

Can you think of a time when you acted on advice and it didn't turn out well?

Extra Insight

Ramoth-gilead was a border city between Aram and Israel.

This week we've focused on surrender. We found that we must humbly submit to God's way. Elisha accepted a call to leave his farming job to pursue full-time prophetic training. When God graciously intervened to help Israel in battle, the leaders accepted His help and followed His instructions. From Naboth's story, we learned that when life doesn't make sense, we can choose to accept the way God does things as we wrestle to reconcile our theology and reality. Today we will consider a *danger* when it comes to surrender: *We should not blindly accept advice without vetting those who are giving it.*

Three years have passed since Ahab humbled himself before Yahweh and received the gracious concession that he would not live to see the pronouncements against Israel come to fruition in his lifetime. During these years, Aramean aggression had ceased, but we will see that it will come into play for the people of Israel once more. A new prophet seems to appear out of thin air as we read about Micaiah today. I don't know where Elijah and Elisha were when this was happening, but we will find a consistent message coming from God's prophets.

Read 1 Kings 22:1-9 and answer the following questions:

How many years did Aram (Syria) and Israel have peace? (v. 1)

Who came to visit King Ahab of Israel? (v. 2)

Over what were they planning to go to war? (vv. 3-4)

What did King Jehoshaphat suggest they do first, and what did he suggest after Ahab took action? (vv. 5, 7)

What did Ahab think about consulting the prophet of Yahweh? (vv. 8-10)

Extra Insight

Micaiah's name means "Who is Like Yahweh?"[13]

Before we continue the story, let's unpack a few things.

It's important to note that while the presenting problem found in this chapter is war with Aram, the issue goes much deeper. Remember that Elijah's name means "Yahweh is my God." We see that the battle over his name still rages: Will Israel continue to waver between serving many gods, or will they listen to Yahweh alone? Is Yahweh the one and only God? Does His Word always come true? Whose counsel will Israel ultimately act on? For that matter, whose counsel will *we* ultimately act on? These are the questions for us to keep in mind as we continue exploring today's passage.

It's also helpful for us to understand the characters and their relationships. King Jehoshaphat—who is king of the Southern Kingdom of Judah—enters the scene with little introduction. You'll recall that the United Kingdom of Israel had been split into two kingdoms since the time of Rehoboam and Jeroboam. Although many passages in 1 Kings mention the long war between these two kingdoms (see 14:30; 15:6-7; and chapters 16–22), "the precise circumstances in which peace was re-established between Judah and Israel . . . are not described."[14] Still, here we see that Jehoshaphat, king of Judah, visited Ahab, king of Israel, as a friend.

Here are some fast facts about King Jehoshaphat:

- He was the king of Judah and the son of King Asa, who was a follower of Yahweh with a good reputation.
- He became king at thirty-five years old and ruled for twenty-five years, with God giving him rest and favor during his rule.

- Jehoshaphat's son Jehoram was married to Ahab's daughter Athaliah (2 Kings 8:18; 2 Chronicles 18:1).
- Though he had flaws, such as the bad judgment in making an alliance with King Ahab of Israel, he was mostly known as a pious, God-fearing king.

So, after being divided for many years, here we find an alliance between the two kingdoms and kings; yet we see a difference in their approach to going to war. Jehoshaphat suggested they seek God's guidance through prophets before making a decision. The fact that he specifically asked for a prophet of Yahweh leads us to the assumption that the other prophets were not as devout or trustworthy as he would have liked. Commentators disagree on the identity of these prophets. Here are a few possibilities:

- leftover and/or new prophets of Baal after the four hundred were killed on Mount Carmel;
- the four hundred prophets of Asherah who were not killed on Mount Carmel; and
- prophets of Yahweh who blended different religious beliefs, diluting pure worship in the way of Jereboam, who set up golden calves and new rules of worship.

Whoever these prophets were, Jehoshaphat sensed that something was fishy. Perhaps he noticed their desire to say whatever it seemed the kings wanted to hear. In any case, he asked for a true prophet of Yahweh.

Ahab hated Micaiah because he delivered blunt words that usually were not sunshine and roses. We might be quick to judge Ahab, but the truth is that we tend to like it when people tell us that circumstances will be easy or that we shouldn't feel convicted. One commentator pointed out that sometimes it seems that Christians today are drifting back to an Ahab mind-set—not hostile to God's Word but perhaps embarrassed by it.[15]

Have you noticed a shift among Christians today toward more of a feel-good message? If so, in what ways?

As we saw yesterday, we need a clear view of God. This means we must accept His grace and His judgment. Ahab wanted the God who makes concessions for humility but not the Lord who might prevent him from going into a battle he was itching to fight.

Scan 1 Kings 22:10-28, or read the summary points below, to see what happens next in today's royal encounter. Then answer the question that follows.

- All of the four hundred prophets prophesied victory against Aram, including Zedekiah, who grabbed some iron horns and said they would gore the Arameans to death. (vv. 10-12)
- Meanwhile the messenger who went to fetch Micaiah said he should agree with the other prophets and say good things. Micaiah replied that he would say only what God told him to say. (vv. 13-14)
- At first Micaiah said sarcastically that they could go up and be victorious, but Ahab pressed him to tell the truth. (vv. 15-16)
- Then Micaiah told them about a vision that revealed that a lying spirit was in the mouth of Ahab's prophets so that he would go into battle and be killed. (vv. 17-23)
- Zedekiah slapped Micaiah, and Ahab ordered Micaiah arrested until Ahab returned safely from battle. (vv. 24-27)
- Micaiah claimed that the king would die and not return or else God had not spoken through him. (v. 28)

Without reading any further, what do you think King Ahab and King Jehoshaphat chose to do after Micaiah told them that going into battle would mean defeat for the army and death for Ahab?

Now Read 1 Kings 22:29-40. What surprises you—or does not surprise you—about the events that happened next?

Extra Insight

The threshing floor where the prophets were parading their scenes of victory was an open space created for agricultural purposes.[16]

It may surprise us that the faithful King Jehoshaphat from Judah disregarded Micaiah's message! He called for a prophet of Yahweh but then rejected his message. He listened to the majority voice instead of God's voice.

This can happen to us too. Rather than impulsively accept the loudest voices, the popular voices, or the most convenient voices, we must study, seek, pray, and wrestle to discern God's voice in each situation we encounter. Then we act. Of course, this is easier said than done.

Yet this is the way God often works—asking one man or woman to listen for His voice and then stand up and go against the crowd. The great revivals in history began when one teenager stood up and confessed sin; one person inspired spiritual awakening; or one individual such as Charles Spurgeon, Jonathan Edwards, or John Wesley began to preach God's Word with power and passion.

Where is God calling you to listen to His voice even when others around you are accepting counterfeits?

The other prophets gave a counterfeit message that felt good. Counterfeits often are more desirous in the moment but ultimately do not deliver. They promise what only the true God can provide. The false prophets promised victory, but only God can give that. And in this instance God said through Micaiah that defeat was sure if they went into battle.

Instead of listening to Micaiah, Ahab wavered—as his life's track record revealed he was prone to do. He chose to go into battle, and yet he tried to disguise himself. Perhaps he thought that just in case Micaiah's message had any merit, he would cover his bases and outwit Yahweh. Ahab couldn't, and neither can we.

Some things we should always surrender to, such as God's way, God's instructions, and God's grace. Other things we should never yield to, such as counterfeits—things that lead us away from wholehearted living for God. Likely, our counterfeits do not look like false prophets walking around on a threshing floor carrying iron horns and promising victory!

What counterfeits of mainstream culture must we guard against in order to listen to God's voice?

There are not any right or wrong answers here. We may be tempted by very different things. Here are a few counterfeits in our Western culture that come to my mind:

- **The love of money**. Money in itself is not bad, but when we depend on it instead of God for security, it can gain counterfeit status in our lives.

> We must study, seek, pray, and wrestle to discern God's voice in each situation we encounter. Then we act.

- **Status**. Things such as our jobs, our spouses' jobs, our notoriety, and our reputations can become things we look to for our identity and value. Even our role in ministry can become an obsession that overtakes our simple love for Jesus.
- **Appearance**. There is nothing wrong with looking our best, but we must not cross the line into elevating our appearance (how we look and what we wear) above our relationship with God.
- **Hobbies**. If online games, social media, movies, television shows, sports we watch or play, or other hobbies get out of hand, we might find ourselves looking to something other than God to satisfy us.
- **Food or drink**. When we look in the refrigerator or pantry to fill the ache inside, we will only find regret or addiction rather than fulfillment.

These things are not inherently bad; they just are not to take God's place in our hearts. Counterfeits make great promises, but only our God can deliver peace to satisfy the longing in our souls. How can we identify the counterfeits in our lives? By considering our time, money, mental energy, and talents and asking ourselves this question: Is *there anything I have elevated above God in my heart*?

Is there anything you have elevated above God in your heart?
Ask God to show you any area where He is calling you to renew your commitment to Him as first in your life, and write a short prayer of response below:

The way to replace counterfeits with the real thing starts with focusing on falling in love with God. No behavior modification plan or elimination program will get at the heart of the issue. Instead we must bring our sin to God with humility, confessing our counterfeits and mourning over them. Then God does a transforming work in our hearts that only He can do.

Today we have learned that we must be careful with surrender, rooting it in God's Word rather than in the voices of our culture. Ahab listened to the wrong voices. He submitted to the counsel of his wicked wife, Jezebel. He acted on the words of prophets who told him only what he wanted to hear. While he had a brief encounter with humility before God, he ultimately chose to walk into the battle that would bring his death just as God said would happen. When the chariot where Ahab died was cleaned, dogs licked his blood just as Elijah had prophesied. While Elijah wasn't center stage in today's lesson, we see the words of his prophecy coming to fruition as we wrap up this week's lesson. We can't help noticing that God's Word always comes true. It never returns void. This is why we study it, pray it, and ask God's Spirit to help us surrender to it and apply it. Let's end our time today doing just that—asking God to help us surrender and act on His Word.

Talk with God

Pray that God will help you surrender to His Word and His way, even when it goes against your reason and emotion. The wise king Solomon penned these words that have helped me on many occasions with my own cognitive dissonance: "Accept the way God does things, / for who can straighten what he has made crooked?" (Ecclesiastes 7:13). Ask God to give you wisdom and discernment to accept His way over the subtle promises of counterfeits.

Weekly Wrap-Up

Take a moment to review what we've studied this week. Flip back through the lessons and write below an insight from each day that you would like to apply in your life. (Feel free to summarize in your own words or copy an excerpt.)

Day 1: Clarity

_____

_____

Day 2: Knowing God

_____

_____

Day 3: It's Not Fair

_____

_____

Day 4: The Power of Humility

_____

_____

Day 5: Careful Surrender

_____

_____

VIDEO VIEWER GUIDE: WEEK 4

Through surrender we find greater _____ with God.

1 Kings 20:13—Prophet predicts victory for King Ahab

Psalm 37:23—The Lord delights in the details of our lives

Humility brings out God's _____ for everyone.

1 Kings 21:24-29—Ahab repents and God relents

Psalm 51:17—God will not reject a broken and repentant heart

James 4:6—God gives grace to the humble

When we can't reconcile our _____ with our _____, we have to accept and surrender to our gracious God.

1 Kings 21:1-4—Naboth refuses to sell his vineyard

Ecclesiastes 7:13—Who can straighten what God has made crooked?

We can find glimpses of _____ even in the most difficult of circumstances.

James 5:10-11—Patience in suffering

2 Corinthians 12:8-10—God's grace is sufficient

Week 5

Mentoring

2 Kings 1–2

Memory Verse

Never let loyalty and kindness leave you!
Tie them around your neck as a reminder.
Write them deep within your heart.
(Proverbs 3:3)

DAY 1: IS THERE NO GOD?

Weekly Reading Plan

Read 2 Kings 9-17

Today's Scripture Focus

2 Kings 1:1-8

For the past four weeks, we've witnessed some of Elijah's habits that brought him spiritual stamina. His journey began with prayer. He sought God in prayer and believed God's word given to him regarding a drought. Like us, he had to persevere in prayer and believe God when life took confusing turns such as the drying up of the brook and the death of the widow's son.

Next Elijah came to a mountaintop season where we watched him make wise choices. He chose not to accept King Ahab's label as the troubler of Israel, and he sorted out fact from fiction by challenging the counterfeit gods of his day to a contest on Mount Carmel. We saw in Elijah's life that our choices do matter. Decisions must be made each day about how we will spend our thoughts, time, energy, and resources. Elijah clung to God, and we can make similar choices when we rely on God's Spirit to guide us.

When things didn't turn out as Elijah expected and the tide of culture continued toward sin and counterfeits, he ran away. We all experience confusing circumstances that don't meet our expectations. From Elijah we discovered the importance of soul care during weary seasons. Elijah slept and ate, and then found God in the stillness. Productivity can be a god in our culture, and we must learn to allow God to restore us so that we can continue to faithfully serve Him.

Last week in our study we found that surrender is important if we are to keep running the race of faith with endurance. Like Elisha, we must accept God's unique call and say no to some things in order to say yes to God.

This week we will focus on Elijah's intentional mentoring of his assistant, Elisha. The primary way he did this was to lead by example. We've now moved from 1 Kings to 2 Kings, but Elijah continues to dominate the narrative; and as we will see in the opening verses, Elijah grows even bolder with time. His prayers, choices, soul care, and surrender have given him stamina to end his ministry, which was deeply rooted in a relationship with God.

Read 2 Kings 1:1-8 and answer the multiple-choice questions that follow by circling the correct letter:

1. After King Ahab died, this country rebelled against Israel:

　A. Ekron

　 B. Moab

　C. Syria

Extra Insight

The Philistine god Baal-zebub of Ekron literally means "lord of the flies," but scholars know little else about this local god.[1]

2. Ahab's son became the new king and his name was:

A. Joram

B. Jehoshaphat

C. Ahaziah

3. After the king injured himself in a fall, he sent messengers to Ekron to consult this god:

A. Baal-zebub

B. Asherah

C. Baal-melqart

4. The angel of the Lord told Elijah to confront the messengers with this message: (circle all letters that apply)

A. Is there no god in Israel?

B. Why are you going to Baal-zebub?

C. You will surely die because you did this.

5. The messengers returned to the king with Elijah's message, and this is how they described Elijah:

A. A bald man

B. A hairy man

C. A fat man

What, if anything, stands out to you about this encounter?

Personally, I was intrigued that God used an angel of the Lord to speak to Elijah. I'm always amazed by how sure the prophets were of their messages, because I often struggle to discern the voice of the Holy Spirit. Sometimes I think God is guiding me to do things such as talk to a certain person about something, make a decision to say yes or no to something, or spend my time or money a certain way. But then I often second-guess myself, wondering if that was really God guiding me or if I was making it up in my head. Have you ever struggled like that?

Answers: 1. B 2. C 3. A 4. A, B, C 5. B

Typically, God spoke directly to the prophets, but here we found an angel of the Lord appeared to Elijah with supernatural information. There was no mistaking Elijah's assignment. The word angel means "messenger." Ahaziah sent messengers to a counterfeit god, but Yahweh sent a very real messenger to instruct Elijah to intervene.

This week in our study old characters are replaced with new ones, but similar themes of spiritual stamina continue. There is a new king on the throne named Ahaziah, but he continues the pattern of rebellion set by his father, Ahab. As we seek to make connections between these foreign names and cultural customs that are very different from our own, we must continually reflect on our lives and decisions. One commentator said it this way: "Even as the story renews itself through new characters, settings, and events, readers are challenged to renew their lives by removing the aspects of the characters that may lead to disaster in their own eras."[3] In other words, the characters and details may have changed, but it's the same old story. Ahaziah's bad decision led to disaster when he sought counterfeits instead of Yahweh.

What principle do we learn from the repetition of themes found in Second Kings?

What we find in today's verses is much more than the clash of a king and a prophet. It is the clash of counterfeits and reality. The king represents an entire royal line and the people who follow its lead by clinging to false gods rather than Yahweh. It is a clash of worldviews. This is the same battle Elijah had fought at Mount Carmel: *Is Yahweh or Baal the real God—with power and authority over weather, sickness, life, and death?* Just as the new king of Israel has adopted the futile faith of his father, we must reflect on our own tendencies to look to counterfeits when we are in trouble.

What has been the most recent troubling circumstance in your life? It could be something small such as an appliance breaking or something big such as a medical diagnosis or job loss.

Our behavior reveals what we truly believe.

Where did you look for comfort and/or wisdom as you dealt with this circumstance?

King Ahaziah had a life-threatening accident, falling from an upper room and sustaining an injury. In the culture of Ahaziah's day, the worldview took a much more mystical and spiritual tone than the naturalism that pervades our society. Though we know very little about Baal-zebub or the religion of Ekron, which was a Philistine city, the details of this specific deity are inconsequential; for the main point Elijah is making refers to the fact that he sought help apart from Yahweh. The problem was disregard for Yahweh as the only legitimate source of help for healing.

Similarly, the application for us is that we must consider what we do when difficulties come our way. Our behavior reveals what we truly believe. Do we believe God cares and is powerful enough to help us? Our temptation does not usually lie in calling out to false deities of surrounding nations. Instead, we tend to turn to counterfeits that reflect our more naturalist and humanist culture.

What are some things that people turn to for help instead of God when something bad happens in their lives? List below a few that come to mind:

I thought of things such as reason or logic, people, human systems, and money. These things are not inherently wrong, as Baal-zebub was; but when we allow them to take the place of God as the "savior" in our circumstances or lives, we are placing our trust in human strength. We must learn to utilize the things of the world without allowing them to become idols in our lives. One of the clearest indicators of where our faith is truly rooted is what we do when change or difficulty strikes. Where do we turn first when the bottom falls out of our lives? Ahaziah turned to the God of Ekron. Seasons of change often reveal our true spiritual temperament. Another way to put it is that who we really are comes out when we are squeezed.

Elijah's message to the king was "Is there no God in Israel?" For us the questions might be "Is Jesus Lord of everything? Can He truly make a difference in whatever I am going through?"

As a pastor's wife for over two decades, I've been surprised when some people who appeared spiritually strong on the outside fell apart and didn't cling to God when difficulties came into their lives. It is heartbreaking to watch those you love look for comfort in alcohol, sexual relationships, or material possessions when you know that crying out to God is the only thing that will bring them true comfort.

What happened with the kings of Israel was a spiritual drift from uncompromising faith in the God who created them. While former kings such as David and Solomon left a legacy of faith, those who came after them watered down the message and laws of God. They tolerated foreign gods and then eventually added the worship of those gods to their spiritual practices. Yet Yahweh faithfully sent prophets such as Elijah and Elisha to call them back. We must guard against a similar tendency to drift.

Read Hebrews 2:1 below, and underline the verbs:

So we must listen very carefully to the truth we have heard, or we may drift away from it.

According to this verse, listening carefully directly correlates to helping us stay aligned with truth. Ahab, Ahaziah, and the people in their kingdom did not pay attention to God's messages, and, consequently, they drifted away from the truth. When he injured himself, Ahaziah turned immediately to a counterfeit god.

When tragedies have arisen in my life, I have responded in different ways depending on the spiritual temperature of my life. When I went through a miscarriage and infertility, I struggled with bitterness, isolation, and self-pity. I watched a lot of television to numb my pain. As God continued to grow my faith, I responded differently when one of our daughters endured a life-threatening health situation when she was five. Born out of desperation, my prayer life grew by leaps and bounds; I prayed as I had never prayed before.

Reflect on a season of difficulty in your life, and describe how you found strength in the Lord when you sought His help:

We must choose where to turn for help when tragedy strikes, but the biggest influence on what we do in those situations is the faith we have nurtured during both the ordinary and good times. If we develop an intimacy with God in the

Who we really are comes out when we are squeezed.

normal routine of life, we are more likely to seek Him first when tragedy strikes. Our deep faith will assure us that He is the source of hope and healing in our seasons of brokenness.

What are some practices that have helped you build spiritual stamina in your life?

For me, participating in Bible studies, developing a more disciplined prayer life, strengthening relationships with my church family, reading God's Word, and listening to sermons all help me to grow deeper roots. At the same time, too much television, excess food or drink or worldly influences, and isolation from Christian community can cause me to drift spiritually. The stakes are high because our actions have consequences.

Ahaziah received a punishment for seeking a counterfeit god: he lost his life. Though we may not lose our lives, nothing good happens when we turn to counterfeits. There are no alternatives to Yahweh as God. This is the lesson we must learn and live. To have spiritual stamina, we cannot put our trust in counterfeits or false gods rooted in human logic or emotion. Only Yahweh is real. He alone can bring healing and hope!

Talk with God

Ask God to help you turn to Him when you need help. Pray the words of Psalm 80:3:

Turn us again to yourself, O God.
Make your face shine down upon us.
Only then will we be saved.

DAY 2: BOLDER WITH TIME

As a child, I had many fears. One of them included talking to people I didn't know. Ordering food, asking for help, or just meeting new people caused me internal anxiety. While I still don't like negotiating or asking for a better deal, I've learned that most people aren't so scary. Life experiences such as dealing with banks and insurance or utility companies have caused me to realize that sometimes you have to ask questions and straighten out mistakes.

My mentor, Deb, is really bold. When I'm out to dinner with her, I always chuckle as she asks the server many questions about the menu and often requests substitutions. She has no problem asking. I always order just what is on the menu with no questions or requests. She also is the queen of making sure that treatment is fair. Once a group from our church went to a leadership conference, and one of the rooms was not in acceptable condition. She didn't flinch in making sure everything was appropriately handled. If I need help standing up for something, Deb is my source for support. By watching Deb, I've learned to be much bolder over time.

Today we will encounter a very bold Elijah. Nearing the end of his life, he showed Elisha an example of a man who is fearless when it comes to people. This is not the Elijah cowering or regrouping in the wilderness when Jezebel threatened him. His faith has grown to be unshakable. Elisha was watching Elijah, and we see later in 2 Kings that he came to emulate his mentor's bold faith.

Yesterday we learned that when King Ahaziah's messengers described the man who had said, "Is there no God in Israel?" he immediately knew it was Elijah. Ahaziah was familiar with Elijah—the man his father had called the troubler of Israel (1 Kings 18:17). Before we pick up where we left off, let's take a moment to consider what was going on with God's people around this time period as the transition from Elijah to Elisha as Israel's prophet was taking place.

After King Ahab died, his son Ahaziah found himself smack-dab in the middle of some serious problems! As we've learned, the nation of Moab had rebelled (2 Kings 1:1); and according to the Moabite Stone, an inscribed monument from this time in history, the king of Moab captured Israelite lands as well as refused to pay tribute.[6] Not only was Moab a problem, but so was Aram. You'll recall from our study last week that King Ben-hadad from Aram had attacked Israel. With Yahweh's help the nation of Israel defeated Aram, but all of the Israelite victories would turn out to be short lived. After Ben-hadad, Hazael would become king of Aram, and he would exert his authority throughout the land, making Israel pay tribute and whittling down their army and land. To put it simply, it was a time of unrest and uncertainty as Israel faced ongoing conflict with neighboring kingdoms!

Ahaziah reigned on the throne in Israel only two years. Not only did he have the external pressures of Moab and Syria but he also faced a downturn in the economy. Without a lasting alliance with King Jehoshaphat of Judah, the nation of Israel diminished from the wealth it enjoyed under Ahab. Then Ahaziah fell and was injured. Life certainly was no picnic for him! He had problems weighing on him at every turn; and like his father before him, he did not see Yahweh's

Extra Insight

Second Kings 1:8 tells us that Elijah was a hairy man with a leather belt around his waist. The language suggests either that he wore hairy clothes or that he was hairy beyond the traditional long beard customary of Israelite culture.[5]

prophet Elijah as a source of help. Instead, Elijah became a target and a source of blame for Ahaziah's many problems.

A similar thing can happen to us when our perspective becomes skewed: we can start to view the source of our help and strength with disdain. Ahaziah could have chosen to repent and depend on Yahweh, but instead he tried to control and capture Elijah. Let's see how Elijah responded to Ahaziah's methods of intimidation.

Read 2 Kings 1:9-18, and either draw or write below what happened in the three attempts Ahaziah made to summon Elijah:

1.

2.

3.

How would you describe Elijah's response in these accounts?

In verses 16-17, Elijah's bold response essentially delivered his life's message once again, which was to prove the truth of the meaning of his name: *Yahweh is my God.* We find this pattern throughout Elijah's ministry:

- Yahweh is greater than Baal. (1 Kings 17–19)
- Yahweh is Lord of the hills and the valleys. (1 Kings 20)
- Yahweh punishes sin and directs battles. (1 Kings 21–22)

This is the message that Elijah taught again and again, applying it in each new situation. In the same way, our message today is still that Yahweh is God—that He is all-sufficient—both holy and merciful, powerful and compassionate.

He loves us and calls us to turn away from our sin and toward Him. He offers us new life through the blood of His Son and power over sin through the Holy Spirit.

How have you seen our all-sufficient God working in your life lately (through circumstances, His Word, power over sin, people, etc.)?

Because of Elijah's boldness, everyone could see where the real power resides—not in Baal-zebub but in Yahweh alone.

Read Proverbs 28:1 in the margin. How does this verse describe the Elijah we see in today's text?

The wicked run away when no one is chasing them,
*   but the godly are as bold as lions.*
*   (Proverbs 28:1)*

Now, let me offer a word of explanation here. We all have different tendencies and personality types. My mentor, Deb, is naturally bold, while I tend to have more of a bent toward shyness (despite the fact that I teach before large audiences). God doesn't put His stamp of approval on one personality type over another. He knit us together in our mothers' wombs, making each of us unique. Yet whether we are more introverted or extroverted, we all can develop a bolder faith. As we grow in godliness, our "boldness" will increase—whether it's more of a quiet or a loud nature; but in either case, our trust in God will be steadfast and secure.

Put an X on the line below to indicate how you are responding to the problems in your life right now:

Fearful   Sometimes fearful   Fairly bold   Bold as a lion

_____

Whatever your personality type may be and wherever you are on this scale right now, you can move closer to being bold as a lion in your faith. Remember, having boldness does not mean that we are loud and obnoxious. In fact, the Hebrew word used in Proverbs 28:1 is *batach*, which most often is translated "trust." It means:

- to trust, trust in;
- to have confidence, be confident;

Whatever your personality type . . . you can move closer to being bold as a lion in your faith.

- to be bold; and
- to be secure.[7]

Being bold, then, is trusting in God. Elijah displayed this trust when he didn't fear an army of fifty men. He trusted God more than what his eyes could see, and he called down fire on those seeking to capture him.

Elijah's response of calling down fire on his opponents might cause us some confusion in light of a passage found in the New Testament.

Read Luke 9:51-56 in the margin. How did Jesus differ from Elijah when it came to calling down fire?

What is different about this New Testament situation compared to what was happening to Elijah?

51As the time drew near for him to ascend to heaven, Jesus resolutely set out for Jerusalem. 52He sent messengers ahead to a Samaritan village to prepare for his arrival. 53But the people of the village did not welcome Jesus because he was on his way to Jerusalem. 54When James and John saw this, they said to Jesus, "Lord, should we call down fire from heaven to burn them up?" 55But Jesus turned and rebuked them. 56So they went on to another village.
(Luke 9:51-56)

Jesus rebuked His disciples for wanting a demonstration of fire. I have to wonder if James and John had this account from Elijah's life in mind when they made their suggestion. What we must understand is that the circumstances were different. In Elijah's case, God was protecting His Word and His servant. One commentator observes, "Elijah acted not out of private vengeance but for the Name of God and such divine judgment is clear in the New Testament also (Heb. 12:29; Rev. 11:5; 2 Thes. 1:7-9)."[8] Elijah was defending himself against attackers, whereas James and John may have wanted to punish those who would not help them.

At first glance, this account from Elijah's life may seem to reveal a scary God who destroys people at will, but this actually is not the case here. We must remember that a prophet was sent by God to speak God's messages, calling His people back into relationship with Him—which was not a palatable message to a broad range of folks! Rather than try to entertain people into listening to God, Elijah simply preached the messages God revealed to him. God gave caution lights and messages of warning, stepping into the role of judge only after Israel repeatedly failed to heed His warnings regarding sin, rebellion, and idolatry.

Elijah faithfully delivered messages of mercy and judgment, and he boldly trusted God more than any threat or intimidation. He called down fire but also relented, sparing the third group as the angel of the Lord instructed him. Elijah was submissive, surrendering to God's voice but no other. One commentator described Elijah as one who did not play by the rules of the king, believing there were no restraints on what was possible for God.[9]

I want to be described that way, don't you? We wish we didn't worry about the opinions of others, fret over the future, or sometimes look to counterfeits to soothe the difficulties of life. But rather than discourage us, I hope Elijah's example encourages us to grow. Like Elijah, we can learn to live with the frame of mind that with God there are no restraints on what is possible!

As you consider all we have learned about Elijah so far in our study, what do you think might have contributed to the boldness we see in him here in 2 Kings 1?

What are some practical steps you might take to live more boldly for God?

Elijah's confidence in God has had low points and high points along the way; but here near the finish line of his earthly race, his faith is bold. He knows where his identity is rooted, and he knows the character of his God. We too will grow bolder over time as we exercise faithful persistence in our prayers, choices, soul care, surrender, and mentoring relationships. I know I am bolder in my faith than I was ten years ago because I've had ten more years of seeing God work. How about you? Sure, we'll likely doubt and struggle on occasion, but still we will develop spiritual stamina over time as we continually seek God rather than counterfeits.

Talk with God

Ask God to replace any fears you may have with boldness. Bring each and every concern you have before God right now, and ask Him to give you a holy boldness in the face of each one.

DAY 3: I WILL NEVER LEAVE YOU

Today's Scripture Focus

Lately I've been traveling with the Aspire Women's Events. An Aspire event is a women's retreat packed into one evening full of laughter, learning, stories, and music. At every event, I hear my friend Mia Koehne sing a song called "You

2 Kings 2:1-6

are Not Alone" just before I go on stage to teach from God's Word. As I watch the women in the audience respond to this song, I see many wiping away tears as the message that God is with us resonates so deeply within them.

Mia often shares her testimony, telling how she left her husband and children in search of fulfillment in ungodly things. She finally reached the end of her rope in sin and fell into total despair. About that time, her sister called and reminded her of God's love, boldly asking her, "Are you about done?" Mia broke down, choosing to repent and return to God. Her marriage was restored, and her family was healed.

As I take the stage after Mia's testimony and song, I'm always struck by how God transforms lives—reminding us we are not alone even when we feel that way. God uses us as members of the body of Christ to reach out and remind one another of His hope in the midst of despair.

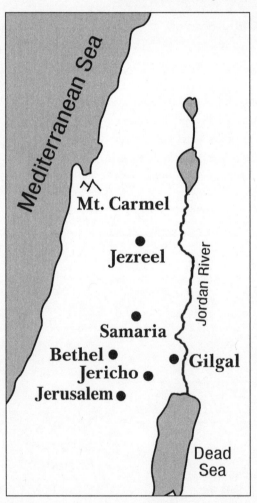

Though Elijah may seem to be a solitary figure in the biblical narrative, we know he mentored Elisha, pouring into Elisha's life with his own example of bold trust in God. Today we will get a glimpse of Elisha's commitment to Elijah. Loyal relationships are an important part of the Christian life. We were not meant to live for God in isolation. While we may have seasons of aloneness, as Elijah experienced at the Kerith Brook, we also will have times when God tells us to pour our lives into others.

God spoke to Elijah in a still small voice, telling him to anoint Elisha and find his people; and in our text for today, we find proof that Elijah obeyed God's command.

Read 2 Kings 2:1-6, and draw arrows on the map to show the path of Elijah and Elisha's journey.

What did Elisha say each time Elijah told him to stay?

Elijah was in the home stretch of his ministry. Everyone seemed to know that Elijah soon would be taken up to God. Commentators are unsure why Elijah asked Elisha to stay at Bethel and Jericho instead of going with him, but we see that Elisha was committed to staying with his master. One commentator points out, "The verb 'leave' has the force of 'abandon.'"[10] It's clear that the mentor and mentee did not have a casual relationship but a committed one.

This kind of relationship takes time, intentionality, and commitment through different seasons of life. My mentor, Deb, has been in my life for twenty years and has seen me at my lowest and highest moments. She has prayed with me, sat with me in hospital rooms, and walked me through the years of parenting teenagers. Deb also has been there to celebrate graduations, good news, and holidays. We don't have constraints, expectations, or rules for each other but are committed to each other through thick and thin. When I feel alone, as we all do from time to time, God often reminds me of Deb and the gift of love and loyalty we share. My hope and prayer is that you either have a mentor in your life or will begin prayerfully seeking one.

Whether or not you use the word *mentor* to describe her, who is someone you look up to as a woman of faith who can help you in a crisis and show up for the big celebrations in your life (births, graduations, weddings)?

In today's text, we see that Elisha was committed to Elijah. This is an example of a mentee being loyal and faithful to a mentor.

Whether or not a name came to mind for the above question, is there someone for whom you could begin "showing up" in order to form a deeper relationship?

I have had a few women ask me to "mentor" them. Although I am okay with setting up regular meetings, sometimes that can feel strained or forced. Rather than meeting at a certain time and place, Deb and I have preferred to do life and ministry together—working alongside each other in children's and youth ministry and getting together after church (because neither of us is the best planner!). Because we were serving together in ministry, we saw each other regularly, which naturally resulted in us making other plans together.

If you want a close relationship with a mentor, consider these ideas:

- Serve as an apprentice or helper in the ministry where she serves.
- Show up at church often so you will have a regular touchpoint with her.
- Join the Bible study or small group that she leads or attends.
- Invite her for a meal or coffee with no agenda.

The regular touchpoints that Deb and I had in ministry led to fun brainstorming sessions, vacation plans, holiday dinners, and meals—including those we took to each other during challenging times. Because we knew what was going on in each other's lives, we were able to support each other through the highs and lows. My relationship with Deb has brought me spiritual stamina in many ways. She has helped me keep going when I've wanted to quit. Her prayers and encouraging words have been life-giving to me—and she would say the same.

Both of us would admit that there have been times when we have chosen to participate in something for no other reason than to be there for the other. Sometimes I haven't felt like going to a party, baby shower, or other event; but when I learned Deb was in charge of it, I showed up because I love her. She has made sacrifices with her time for me as well, attending events that were important to me. That is what commitment looks like. We show up even when we don't feel like it because we are committed.

Never let loyalty and kindness leave you! Tie them around your neck as a reminder. Write them deep within your heart. Then you will find favor with both God and people, and you will earn a good reputation.
(Proverbs 3:3-4)

Read Proverbs 3:3-4 in the margin, and write the command and the promise in your own words:

Command: Never _____

Promise: Then you will _____

Though we should always be open to new relationships and friendships, we should be careful to treasure the history we have with loyal friends. It can be easy to shift away from people when relationships get hard and move on to new people. The problem is that eventually those people's flaws will come out too, and so we're right back in the same situation. Loyalty and longevity of relationships are some things I have grown to appreciate more with time.

Take a moment to write a text, email, or card to a few people with whom you have shared a long history of loyalty, telling them how much you treasure them and are committed to them. Or if you cannot do it now, write their names below as a reminder to follow through on this action plan:

Elisha's commitment to Elijah reminds me of the biblical story of Ruth and Naomi. After Naomi's husband and two sons died while in the land of Moab, Naomi asked her daughters-in-law, Orpah and Ruth, not to travel back with her to her homeland of Israel. She was bitter and grieving and asked them to return to their families.

Read Ruth 1:6-18. What did Naomi's daughters-in-law decide to do?

Orpah:

Ruth:

Orpah returned to her family, but Ruth determined not to leave Naomi. She said, "Don't ask me to leave you and turn back. Wherever you go, I will go; wherever you live, I will live. Your people will be my people, and your God will be my God" (Ruth 1:16).

Naomi told Ruth to return to her family, and Elijah asked Elisha to stay behind. In each case the younger person did not listen to the mentor but stayed close through a challenging season. We too need discernment to know when to stay with those who are experiencing difficult times even if they say they don't need us.

Can you recall a time when you told people you didn't need a meal, some help, or their presence but they showed up anyway? Describe anything that comes to mind:

Though we should always be open to new relationships and friendships, we should be careful to treasure the history we have with loyal friends.

Is the Holy Spirit nudging you to come alongside someone facing a difficult situation in a tangible way, even if the person has not asked for this? Write any names and ideas that come to mind below:

The Lord has been reminding me of a sweet friend who has faced health challenge after health challenge. She hates needing so much help and often will not ask for it. I need to make time to go and sit with her, take her a meal, and remind her that she is not alone.

While Elijah and Elisha shared a close relationship, there also was a larger community of prophets as well. As we learned earlier in our study, Elijah told God at Mount Sinai that he alone was left as the only follower of Yahweh; and God told him there were seven thousand others who had not bowed their knee to Baal. God then instructed Elijah to go back the way he had come and find these people (1 Kings 19:15, 19). We find the dynamic of community here in 2 Kings 2 as well.

Reread 2 Kings 2:3, 5. What did the prophets from Bethel and Jericho say to Elisha?

What was Elisha's response each time?

Here we find that groups of prophets existed in both Jericho and Bethel, and they seemed familiar with Elijah and Elisha since they kept telling Elisha that his master was going to be taken away. These groups of prophets served Yahweh as well, and it seemed they wanted to prepare Elisha for his master's earthly departure. While we cannot be close friends with everyone, we too have a larger community of faith. Our church families can be a source of support for us just as the groups of prophets were for Elisha and Elijah.

Of course, being in community also means we may step on one another's toes now and then. Elisha didn't like being told what he already knew about his master being taken. We might experience a similar irritation when people repeatedly tell us things we already know, especially when it concerns hard truths. We always should be sensitive when people are grieving or enduring difficult times. Just because something is true does not mean we are obligated to say it. For example, it's true "that God causes everything to work together for the good of those who love God and are called according to his purpose" (Romans 8:28), but this verse is not something I would say to someone who was just diagnosed with cancer.

Read Proverbs 25:20 in the margin. What principle do we learn from this verse?

Singing cheerful songs to a person with a heavy heart is like taking someone's coat in cold weather or pouring vinegar in a wound.
(Proverbs 25:20)

While the prophets weren't singing songs to Elisha, they were reminding him of an impending loss of which he was well aware. We should consider what *not* to say as well as what to say when people are facing hardship or loss.

What are some things others have said to you when you were hurting that may have been true but were not helpful?

When we don't know what to say, we sometimes say things that hurt rather than help, such as:

- God is still on the throne.
- It's probably for the best.
- God knows what He is doing.
- It could have been worse.
- They are better off now.
- God must have known you can handle this.
- I know what you are going through.
- God is preparing you for something.

I'm reminded of the friends of Job, who did not sin until they started talking. Sometimes the best thing we can do is tell someone we are sorry, we are praying for them, and we love them.

As Elijah neared the end of his life, he was not alone. Elisha never abandoned him. Like my friend Mia's song, we are not alone either—even if we may feel that way. Remember that God has given us the gift of community—whether we find it through our family, church community, friends, or a mentor/mentee relationship. And even if we do not have a physical person with us, God has promised never to leave us!

Sometimes the best thing we can do is tell someone we are sorry, we are praying for them, and we love them.

"So be strong and courageous! Do not be afraid and do not panic before them. For the Lord your God will personally go ahead of you. He will neither fail you nor abandon you."

(Deuteronomy 31:6)

"May the Lord our God be with us as he was with our ancestors; may he never leave us or abandon us."

(1 Kings 8:57)

Don't love money; be satisfied with what you have. For God has said,

"I will never fail you.
 I will never abandon you."

(Hebrews 13:5)

Talk with God

Thank God for the people in your life, and pray for anyone you know who is experiencing difficulty today. Ask God to give you the right words to tell them that you are coming alongside them in love and prayer.

DAY 4: CHARIOTS OF FIRE

Today's Scripture Focus

2 Kings 2:7-14

Extra Insight

"The contrast between the deaths of Elijah and his enemies could hardly be any more stark. Elijah, the faithful servant of God, ascends to heaven. Ahab and Jezebel, the sworn enemies of Yahwism and the prophets, die at the hands of their foes."[11]

What is your first reaction when you read the title of today's lesson? I'll admit my mind recalls the movie by the same title, which is about two runners in the 1924 Olympics. One of the runners was a Jewish man named Ben Abrahams, and the other was Eric Liddell, a devout Christian Scotsman whose parents were missionaries in China. His strong faith prohibited him from running on Sundays as he honored the Sabbath with rest. This created a tension for him when the Olympic race he prepared for was scheduled for a Sunday. He is well known for saying, "God made me fast, and when I run, I feel His pleasure."[12] He later became a missionary in China himself, but his story inspired many to see that they could use their God-given talent or gift for God's glory.

The movie title was inspired by a poem written by William Blake called *Jerusalem*, which mentions a chariot of fire as an allusion to Elijah in 2 Kings 2. Blake also refers to God's bow, arrows, and spear in addition to the chariot of fire. When Hubert Parry set the poem to music around the time of World War I, it became a patriotic hymn, referring to England as a green and pleasant land. The hymn was sung in the movie and inspired the director to change the name of the movie from *Running* to *Chariots of Fire*.

Let's look back to the original chariot of fire and see what we can learn from Elijah's final moments on earth.

Read 2 Kings 2:7-14, and draw the scene as Elijah is going up in the whirlwind. Include the following:

- **some of the prophets watching from a distance**
- **Elijah**
- **Elisha**
- **Elijah's cloak**
- **the chariot of fire and horses**
- **the whirlwind**

If you really don't like to draw, then feel free to write the names in the appropriate places in the scene. A representation of the parted Jordan River is already in the picture. There isn't a wrong way to do this; just draw as you envision things from your reading of the text!

Extra Insight

The only biblical precedent for Elijah's going was Enoch, who disappeared because God took him (Genesis 5:24).

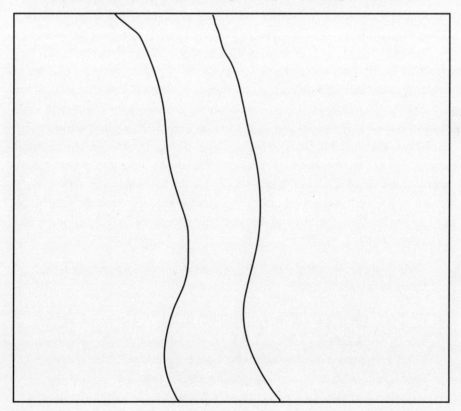

Look again at verse 9. What was Elijah's invitation, and what was Elisha's final request?

Elijah invites Elisha to name one final thing that he can do for him. It's reminiscent of a deathbed scene where someone asks for one last thing from a loved one. And Elijah's open-ended invitation seemed to allow for something that only God could grant. It makes me wonder: If I could ask for one thing from God, what would it be? What would it be for you? Just think about that for a moment, rather than writing anything down.

Elisha didn't ask to be released from his calling or to be given a promise of provision. As one commentator explains, like Solomon asking God for wisdom instead of fame, power, or money, Elisha made a godly request. He asked for a double share, which is one more portion than is normally distributed (Deuteronomy 21:15-17; 1 Samuel 1:5). This was what the firstborn son would expect of a father.[13] Elijah could not guarantee the request, because only Yahweh can bestow the power of the Spirit of God. However, it was a noble request. Elisha longed to do God's work as a prophet with a double share of power from God.

As I read Tim Keller's book *Prayer: Experiencing Awe and Intimacy with God*, I was struck by his remarks about the tone we use when making requests of God. In speaking about the Apostle Paul, Keller notes, "It is remarkable that in all of his writings Paul's prayers for his friends contain no appeals for changes in their circumstances. It is certain that they lived in the midst of many dangers and hardships. They faced persecution, death from disease, oppression by powerful forces, and separation from loved ones."[14] Keller goes on to say that it isn't wrong to ask God for help in tangible ways. We are welcome to do this in many places in Scripture. Even the Lord's Prayer encourages us to ask for daily bread and protection from the evil one. Yet Paul's prayers reveal what he thought was most important.

Read Paul's prayer for the church in Ephesus below, and underline the things he asked God for:

Ever since I first heard of your strong faith in the Lord Jesus and your love for God's people everywhere, I have not stopped thanking God for you. I pray for you constantly, asking God, the glorious Father of our Lord Jesus Christ, to give you spiritual wisdom and insight so that you might grow in your knowledge of God. I pray that your hearts will be flooded with light so that you can understand the confident hope he has given to those he called—his holy people who are his rich and glorious inheritance.

I also pray that you will understand the incredible greatness of God's power for us who believe him. This is the same mighty power that raised Christ from the dead and seated him in the place of honor at God's right hand in the heavenly realms.

(Ephesians 1:15-20)

How would you summarize or describe the kinds of things that Paul was requesting?

Everything Paul prayed for the church in Ephesus had to do with inner life rather than outward circumstances. His requests throughout all of his letters refer to intimacy with God above circumstantial fixes. Paul prayed that others would *know God more.* Similarly, Elisha did not ask Elijah for money, a more reasonable king, a school building or housing for the prophets, or greater fame. Rather, he asked for a double portion of God's Spirit.

This realization caused me to pause and consider the tone of my own prayers. Again, it is not wrong to ask for help and relief from life's aches, but our primary concern should be for our spiritual well-being. So, I turned to my prayer journal of requests where I write what women have asked me to pray for them. I looked at these requests and my own prayers that I have written for my children, and I discovered that the overarching tone of my prayers is for life to get easier for people.

If you have a prayer journal or list, take a moment to review it right now. Or simply recall the content of your recent prayers. What kinds of things are you asking God for?

Whether it is for my family, my friends, or the many women who share prayer requests with me, my prayers often are asking for kids to behave, houses to sell, marriages to get easier, surgeries to go well, jobs to go more smoothly, needs and wants to be provided, and people to be safe. None of these requests is bad, but I long to have a heart that also desires more for us than simply less complicated lives. I want to regularly pray for things such as Paul mentions in Ephesians 1—that we would know God better, that we would understand His love more fully, and that we would have spiritual wisdom and insight, confident hope, and greater understanding of God's mighty power that raised Jesus from the dead.

Write a prayer below focused on the inner life rather than outward circumstances. You can pray for others or for yourself:

Remembering God's power emboldens our prayers.

I want to grow in prayer, don't you? Prayer is vital to our spiritual stamina. Elijah prayed for rain and fire and also talked to God about his discouragement, so we know that we are invited to dialogue with God about anything. However, Elijah's ultimate goal in asking for fire and rain was for Yahweh's people to return to Him, not for their lives to be easier. As we consider our own motives in prayer, may we draw closer to our powerful God who sent down a chariot of fire to accompany his servant to heaven. Remembering God's power emboldens our prayers.

If I'm honest, sometimes my prayers sound like this: "God, if you could, please be with this person...," "God, if you are able, please make the weather right for the wedding," or "God, if you can, please help my daughter on her test." The wimpiness of these prayers is hard for me even to type! But as I refocus on who God is, I am assured that He can do *anything*; He is not limited in power.

Elijah understood that God could stop rain, bring rain, feed him using birds or a poor widow, and rain down fire from heaven. In today's passage we see his mentee, Elisha, demonstrate equally bold faith as he struck the Jordan River with Elijah's cloak and parted the waters in Moses-like fashion. As Paul reminds us in his prayer that we read in Ephesians 1, the same power that raised Jesus from the dead lives in us who believe in Him! In light of this, let's move away from wimpy prayers and begin to ask boldly, as we are led by the Holy Spirit, for our mighty God to do mighty things!

What changes would you like to see in your personal prayer life?

What is one small step you can implement today to begin working toward that goal?

Extra Insight

After his master and father figure was taken up to heaven, Elisha tore his clothing. This was a Hebrew gesture of grief at loss.[15]

Elijah and Elisha asked God for big things. They believed He could accomplish them and watched Him act mightily in the midst of an ungodly culture. Like them, we can ask God to do great things too. We just need to evaluate what is truly great, so that we can seek deeper knowledge of God and spiritual wisdom rather than just an easier life. I remember hearing someone pray this prayer when I was a teenager: "God, break my heart with the things that break yours." God's heart breaks over counterfeits, suffering, and indifference toward Him. Let's continually press on to know God and live in total dependence on Him in the pattern of Elijah!

Contrary to many artists' renderings, the passage we've been exploring today does not put Elijah *in* the chariot of fire. Rather, he ascended in a whirlwind with the chariot of fire beside him. Elijah finished the race of his life well and went out in a blaze of glory. He is an example to each of us.

Read Hebrews 12:1 in the margin. What are some practical ways the Holy Spirit is prompting you to strip off weights that slow you down and run with endurance the race God has set before you?

Therefore, since we are surrounded by such a huge crowd of witnesses to the life of faith, let us strip off every weight that slows us down, especially the sin that so easily trips us up. And let us run with endurance the race God has set before us.

(Hebrews 12:1)

Endurance isn't easy for us. I love to start projects but often get stalled out in the middle. Elijah had some tough moments in the middle too. However, he endured and finished the race God set before Him in a mighty way. Likewise, his mentee Elisha would need endurance at the beginning of his new responsibilities. Whether we are at the beginning of a new season or nearing the end of one, God longs to walk with us through every phase, empowering and strengthening us. If you need endurance to weather a trial, grow in personal spiritual disciplines, or navigate relationships with others, God longs to empower and strengthen you. No matter what season you are experiencing right now, you can gain spiritual stamina as you strip off the weight of sin and pursue God one step at a time.

Talk with God

Ask God to break your heart with the things that break His. Spend some time praying for inner growth and spiritual stamina as you seek to run with endurance the race set before you today.

DAY 5: THE POWER OF PRESSURE

Have you ever looked back on a decision you made and realized you were greatly influenced by the pressure of others around you? I asked my teenage daughter what kind of pressures high school students face from their peers, and she said that the pressures often depend on the friends surrounding the individual. Some students are influenced to drink alcohol or break rules while others might feel stress to fit in by dressing a certain way. Others feel academic or athletic pressures. Then I asked her what she has dealt with in the Christian community of teens she hangs out with on a regular basis. She said that people often don't speak their true feelings because they might get laughed at or criticized. The pressure to fit in causes her to be guarded, not always speaking authentically for fear that she might be publicly shamed. Instead she dialogues in a way that she knows will be accepted and approved.

What were some peer pressures that you remember from your high school years?

I remember feeling pressure to say the right things and look a certain way. Whether others doled out the pressure or I just assumed it myself, shame is a powerful pressure tactic. The shame game, unfortunately, doesn't end in high school.

Do you have any current choices or beliefs that you sense others in your life disagree with or disapprove of?

If you can't think of any right now, are there any times from the past that come to mind?

I have second-guessed myself at the hands of others' disapproval when it comes to my choices regarding parenting decisions (discipline, education, clothing choices), the way our family has handled some medical conditions, how to lead a ministry (Sunday school class, youth group meeting, or Bible study), time management, and money choices. And I'm sure there have been times when I've been on the other side of the equation, too, causing others to second-guess themselves—even if unintentionally.

In her excellent book *Shame Lifter*, Marilyn Hontz shares her personal testimony of battling shame and identifies three different postures we can take toward shame: (1) shame-giver, (2) shame-receiver, and (3) shame-lifter. Neither of the first two postures is desirable. We don't want to be a shame-giver or a shame-receiver, yet sometimes we can find it difficult to move out of the posture of a shame-receiver. I know I tend to be pretty hard on myself. When people tell me that I've done something wrong or done something that has hurt them, shame is usually my first response. I wonder if you have taken on the role of shame-receiver a few too many times as well. Shame can bully us into making decisions contrary to what we know is right. Nothing can rob of us of spiritual stamina like shame.

Yesterday we saw that Elisha had a high spiritual moment when he watched his mentor, Elijah, ascend to heaven in a whirlwind. Then he parted the Jordan River with Elijah's cloak. Then he immediately was tested with pressure from a group of peer prophets.

Read 2 Kings 2:15-18, and answer the following questions:

What did the group of prophets from Jericho initially proclaim when Elisha crossed over the Jordan River? (v. 15)

What did they suggest should be done next? (v. 16a)

Why did they believe a search party was needed? (v. 16b)

What was Elisha's initial response to their suggestion? (v. 16c)

What convinced Elisha to go along with their proposal? (v. 17)

This scenario is puzzling to me. Just a few verses earlier, the prophets from Jericho indicated they knew that Elijah was going to be taken away on that day (2 Kings 2:5). Why, then, would they suggest looking for him? They saw the transfer of power with their own eyes, exclaiming that Elisha now had the power of Elijah, yet they still wanted to double-check to be sure that Elijah was really gone.

On the other hand, Elijah had a reputation for disappearing. In 1 Kings 18:12 we learned that Obadiah wanted confirmation that Elijah would meet Ahab, because he feared Elijah might be carried away by the Spirit of God. Perhaps the prophets wanted to be sure that Elijah hadn't simply been carried off by the Spirit to a different location. Another possibility might be that they believed Elijah was dead but wanted to retrieve his body and properly bury it. One commentator points out how important burial rites were in this time and culture, explaining, "It was important to them to avoid the dishonor of a corpse lying unburied."[16] The concept of someone dying without a burial would have been a foreign concept with no precedent except, perhaps, for Enoch. Genesis 5:23-24 tells us that "Enoch lived 365 years, walking in close fellowship with God. Then one day he disappeared, because God took him."

Ultimately, we don't know the exact motives for the prophets' search. What we do know is that Elijah had not just disappeared. Elisha had watched him ascend into heaven in a whirlwind accompanied by chariots of fire. He knew full well there was no body to be found, but he felt pressured into saying yes to those who wanted to search for Elijah. So, Elisha was shamed into rubber-stamping an action he knew to be futile.

The Hebrew uses a two-word combination to express the prophets' shaming of Elisha. The first word is *patsar*, which means "to press, push,"[17] and the second word is *buwsh*, which means "properly, to pale, i.e. by implication to be ashamed."[18] So the two words together, *patsar buwsh*, mean the prophets pressured Elisha until he felt ashamed. Elisha may have been given a double portion of the Spirit, but he did not yet possess the boldness of his own conviction to stand firm in contradicting his prophetic peers.

Many of us have felt this kind of pressure. It may not have come from a group of coworkers or peers, such as Elisha faced, but we have encountered the words, body language, and tone of others pressing us to do something. One time I limited the number of women in my Bible study because a friend told me she liked a small, committed group. Sometimes the pressure isn't overt; but when we do not comply, subtle hints can seem to be threatening.

In what ways have you encountered or witnessed the pressure of others during the past year?

Social media has been one place where I have watched shame-giving galore. Keyboard courage causes people to say things they might never utter in person. And sometimes the comments continue as each person wants to have the last word. Elisha was no different. After he succumbed to the pressure his fellow prophets put on him and their search proved to be in vain, he said, "I told ya so!" Actually, he said, "Didn't I tell you not to go?" (2 Kings 2:18).

Just as the pressure Elisha faced was not sin, often the pressures we face are not either. They can be wisdom issues or matters of opinion or preference. Whether or not something is a sin issue, we can be pressured into using our time, talents, or treasures in unnecessary ways. Elisha had the spirit of Elijah, but he had not yet fully developed the boldness to stand his ground in the same way as his mentor.

Earlier this year I had the opportunity to go on a trip with some amazing women to a friend's lake house. One day we went out on a boat, and many of the gals had fun jumping off a bridge into the lake. Over the course of the day, everyone on the trip ended up taking the leap except me. While no one pressured me at all, I had a brief moment of wondering if I wanted to be the only one who didn't do it. I quickly concluded that I was confident to be the lone dissenter. The next day several of the gals developed significant bruising from the impact of the water. I felt so bad for them; yet I knew that if I had jumped just to prove I could be adventurous, I might have regretted it. In this case, the ability to stand alone may have saved me from some physical pain!

We all have an inner battle with shame. It may be over something that seems trivial such as jumping off a bridge or a more serious decision with greater consequences. Whether real or perceived, shame threatens all of us from time to time. Often this battle rages first in our minds through our perceptions, judgments, and personal filters. Yet we can learn to become a shame-lifter rather than a shame-giver or shame-receiver, following the example of Jesus.

Read Hebrews 12:2 in the margin, and write below the word that describes what Jesus did with shame:

Jesus *disregarded* shame; and through His blood shed on the cross and our repentance, we can disregard it too. Hebrews 12:1, which we read yesterday, talks about stripping off the sin that weighs us down so that we can run with endurance. Verse 2 gives us the key to the stamina we need in the battle with shame: we keep our eyes on Jesus.

We can learn to become a shame-lifter rather than a shame-giver or shame-receiver.

We do this by keeping our eyes on Jesus, the champion who initiates and perfects our faith. Because of the joy awaiting him, he endured the cross, disregarding its shame. Now he is seated in the place of honor beside God's throne."
(Hebrews 12:2)

What are some practical ways you can keep your eyes on Jesus in your daily life?

Some things that help me refocus and look to Jesus so I can keep running the race of faith include serving alongside others, cultivating relationships with godly friends and mentors, worshiping God alone and with others, setting aside time to rest and reflect, and listening to sermons, podcasts, or radio programs that point me to biblical truth. Did you notice that many of these ideas include other people in the body of Christ? We need others who are racing alongside us so that we can remind one another to keep our focus on Jesus. Because so much of the shame battle is fought in our heads and hearts, we must look to Jesus so that we can emulate Him.

Jesus is our example of the ultimate shame-lifter! He did not assign blame but lifted shame *away* from people. In the same way, as we grow alongside one another, learning from godly mentors as well as sowing into the lives of others, we can help one another lift shame instead of pass it back and forth.

When Elijah was discouraged in the wilderness, God told him to go back the way he had come and find others who worshiped Yahweh. God gave him a special relationship with Elisha as well. Like Elijah, we can learn how to be humble while also being sure of God's message and truth in our lives. This is what it means to have holy boldness—standing confidently in what God has revealed to us without ever being self-righteous or smug.

How is the Lord calling you to a posture of holy boldness in your life right now?

Elisha went on to have a successful ministry. He learned spiritual stamina in his adventures and ultimately developed the boldness of his master, Elijah. Through our relationships with others, we too can grow in spiritual stamina and learn to be shame-lifters. With our eyes on Christ, we can disregard shame and stand confident in our decisions even when others disapprove. And we can be shame-lifters for others, too, just as Jesus was and is for each of us.

Talk with God

Ask God to give you His holy boldness. Take a moment to take stock of anything that is causing you to feel guilt or shame. Lift these things up to God, asking Him to help you learn to disregard shame and keep your eyes on Jesus today.

Weekly Wrap-Up

Take a moment to review what we've studied this week. Flip back through the lessons and write below an insight from each day that you would like to apply in your life. (Feel free to summarize in your own words or copy an excerpt.)

Day 1: Is there no God?

_____

_____

Day 2: Bolder with Time

_____

_____

Day 3: I Will Never Leave You

_____

_____

Day 4: Chariots of Fire

_____

_____

Day 5: The Power of Pressure

_____

_____

VIDEO VIEWER GUIDE: WEEK 5

We need mentors because we all have a tendency to drift toward

_____.

2 Kings 1:1-3—Elijah confronts King Ahaziah

Hebrews 2:1—We must listen carefully to the truth or we may drift from it

In mentoring, much more is _____ than _____.

2 Kings 1:9-10—Elijah calls down fire from heaven

Mentoring requires both parties _____ _____ in each other's lives.

2 Kings 2:1-2—Elijah is taken into heaven

We can _____ people from a distance, but we _____ those close to us.

2 Kings 2:9-14—Elisha inherits a double portion of Elijah's spirit

Week 6

Legacy

Elijah in the Old and New Testaments

Memory Verse

*We will not hide these truths from our children;
we will tell the next generation
about the glorious deeds of the LORD,
about his power and his mighty wonders.*
(Psalm 78:4)

DAY 1: SOWING AND REAPING

When I first read through the books of 1 and 2 Kings in college as a requirement for my Old Testament Survey class, I was astounded at the impact one generation had on the next. Though all of the kings of the Northern Kingdom of Israel were evil, God relentlessly pursued them with prophets such as Elijah. In the Southern Kingdom, some kings worshiped Yahweh and passed on that faith to their sons. This gave me pause to think about my own lineage of faith.

My parents missed the mark of perfection as all parents do. I grew up in a dysfunctional family just as you did, because *all* families are composed of and led by sinners. Still, as I learned about the kings of Israel and Judah, I couldn't help being grateful for my family tree. For all the problems and chaos in our family, my parents shared the gospel with me. They brought me to church, sent me to church camps and retreats, and emphasized the need for a personal relationship with Jesus—even though they did not have the same clarity of message in their own childhood homes. They left a legacy for all who will follow after them. As I reflected on this, I realized with deep gratitude in my heart that, although every individual must personally choose whether or not to follow Christ, my parents laid a firm foundation for me. I decided to write them a letter at this juncture in my life, explaining that I had read the books of First and Second Kings and appreciated their legacy of faith.

Whether or not you have parents and grandparents who provided a godly example, you can be the person who changes your own family tree by passing down a heritage of faith. As we come to our last week of study, we leave the books of First and Second Kings to discover other mentions of Elijah's name in Scripture; and we see that his legacy reached far beyond his own time. Last week we learned that Elijah went up to heaven in a whirlwind, but his name did not disappear from Scripture with the chariots of fire. Throughout our week of study, we will find that Elijah's influence was not limited to his prophetic messages in the nation of Israel.

Remember that after King Solomon's reign, the Jewish nation was divided into the Northern Kingdom of Israel and the Southern Kingdom of Judah. Elijah's ministry focused on the nation of Israel, whose kings were all wicked. Yet today we will find that Elijah wrote a letter to one of the kings of the Southern Kingdom of Judah, and we will see that his message remained the same even with the shift in his audience.

We learned earlier in our study that Ahab (king of Israel) had formed an alliance with Jehoshaphat (king of Judah) and had led him into battle against

Weekly Reading Plan

Read 2 Kings 18-25.

Today's Scripture Focus

2 Chronicles 21:1-11

Extra Insight

"Each Passover, a special cup of wine is filled and put on the seder table. During the Seder, the door of the house is opened and everyone stands to allow Elijah the Prophet…to enter and drink."[1]

the counsel of a prophet of Yahweh named Micaiah. During the battle, Ahab was killed while Jehoshaphat escaped. Though that particular decision of Jehoshaphat to go to war was unwise, 2 Chronicles 20:32 tells us, "Jehoshaphat was a good king, following the ways of his father, Asa. He did what was pleasing in the Lord's sight." Jehoshaphat's downfalls were related to his alliances with kings of Israel; but on the whole, he sought the Lord and trusted in Yahweh during his twenty-five-year reign in Judah.

Read 2 Chronicles 21:1-11 and summarize in a few sentences what happened after Jehoshaphat died:

While Asa influenced his son Jehoshaphat toward trusting Yahweh, Jehoram did not follow his own father's legacy of faith. Instead, he was influenced by his wife. Who was his wife according to 2 Chronicles 21:6?

Since the evil influence of Ahab's family had extended to the Southern Kingdom, Elijah's prophetic ministry also reached across the border with Yahweh's response.

Read Elijah's letter to Jehoram found in 2 Chronicles 21:12-15. Write the good examples Jehoram could have followed in the left-hand column and the bad examples he chose to follow in the right-hand column:

Good Example   Bad Examples

1. David

2.

3.

Other kings of Israel you may recall (see 1 Kings 15–16):

Jehoram had some positive role models in the stories of King David. He also had a godly father, Jehoshaphat, and grandfather, Asa.

As you think about your own family heritage, what are some of the good qualities of your parents and grandparents?

While good examples can be helpful, we find here that they are not enough. Even with the best of role models, individuals can turn away from God and toward sin. Jehoram did just that. However, his decisions did not go unnoticed by Yahweh. God instructed Elijah to write this letter with some heavy pronouncements of judgment.

What did Elijah state would happen to Jehoram's body according to 2 Chronicles 21:15?

Every prophecy Elijah made over the course of his ministry proved true. In fact, this was a requirement for a prophet (see Deuteronomy 18:22). As we will read in the remaining verses of the chapter, Elijah's letter came to life—or shall we say proved itself in death.

Read 2 Chronicles 21:16-20, and record below who was sorry when Jehoram died:

Jehoram's evil actions had consequences. He chose to follow bad influences instead of godly examples. By murdering his own siblings, he angered Yahweh; and the words of Elijah's letter came true. This passage in 2 Chronicles reveals that Elijah didn't just speak messages from God; he wrote them exactly as God directed.

Throughout our study of Elijah's life, we've learned several key concepts related to spiritual stamina:

PRAYER: In Week 1 we saw the power of faithful and faith-filled prayer as Elijah listened to God, pronounced a drought, and relied on God for provision both at the Kerith Brook and from the widow of Sidon.

CHOICES: In Week 2 we saw that Elijah chose to support Obadiah and challenge the prophets of Baal on Mount Carmel. We too make choices that impact our ability to keep going when we grow weary.

SOUL CARE: In Week 3 we saw that when Elijah was broken and discouraged, the Lord ministered to him with food and rest under a broom tree and ultimately spoke to him in a still small voice.

SURRENDER: In Week 4 we saw that while Yahweh's instructions and actions do not always make sense to us, we must learn to trust Him wholeheartedly, accepting both the good and the bad in life.

MENTORING: And in Week 5 we explored the importance of community and mentoring relationships as we grow bolder in faith within the context of relationships.

Which of these key concepts relate to Elijah's letter to King Jehoram found in 2 Chronicles? Put a star beside those that you think connect to today's text.

Your answers may differ from mine, but here are some of my observations. First, I noticed that Jehoram failed to rely on and **pray** to Yahweh but instead was swayed toward idolatry. He also made **choices** that led to his judgment. The people he chose to listen to and allow to **mentor** him led him away from God and toward sin.

I can't imagine any legacy I would want less than that of Jehoram! Who would ever say, "I hope I end up like that guy whose bowels came out because of his disobedience to God"? So, in order to build stamina, we must consider our own spiritual lives.

- What are we doing to develop our prayer lives?
- How do we learn to make godly choices?
- Who can we "get alongside" in order to help us grow?

These are questions we must ask if we want to build spiritual stamina in every season of life. The danger in my life is not that I *desire* to be spiritually flabby and weak. Rather, the danger is neglecting to do what is necessary to avoid that condition. I need discipline and spiritual rhythms in order to build spiritual muscles. Yet I often make excuses for my lack of discipline: "Well, everyone else watches a lot of movies and television"; "I don't spend as much time on social media as so-and-so does"; or "Compared to _____, I read the Bible pretty regularly."

In order to follow in the steps of Elijah, we must consider what seeds we are planting with our time, talents, and treasures.

What are some excuses you have made for your lack of spiritual fitness?

While we likely aren't going to worship idols, kill our siblings, and reject the faith of our parents as King Jehoram did, we are in danger of subtle spiritual dangers. Apathy, time-wasting, and lack of diligence in spiritual rhythms can cause a slow rot in our souls. These habits may not be inherently sinful; but if our spiritual diet consistently contains empty calories, we may find ourselves weak when seasons of life bring challenges.

Read Galatians 6:7-9 in the margin. What principle do we learn from these verses?

As you reflect on what you are planting with your time and resources, what changes do you feel nudged to make that might benefit your spiritual stamina? (Think about rest, time management, your thought life, and soul "junk food.")

Don't be misled—you cannot mock the justice of God. You will always harvest what you plant. Those who live only to satisfy their own sinful nature will harvest decay and death from that sinful nature. But those who live to please the Spirit will harvest everlasting life from the Spirit. So let's not get tired of doing what is good. At just the right time we will reap a harvest of blessing if we don't give up.

(Galatians 6:7-9)

I believe most of us want to leave a legacy of faith to the next generation. We want to be remembered as people of faith, prayer, and wisdom. In order to follow in the steps of Elijah, we must consider what seeds we are planting with our time, talents, and treasures. While we will never choose perfectly in every situation, we can grow in wisdom as we consider the principle of sowing and reaping in our lives. We build a legacy of faith through the good seeds we choose to plant, knowing that some of them will be harvested by future generations.

Talk with God

Ask God to show you any areas where soul "junk food" or time-wasting has had a negative impact on your spiritual stamina. Don't dwell in shame for any bad decisions you've made, but ask God to show you the good seeds He is calling you to plant today.

We build a legacy of faith through the good seeds we choose to plant.

DAY 2: THE FATHER-HEART OF GOD

Throughout our study of Elijah's life, we have seen God calling His wayward people to return to Him. Like a Father calling to His children, God used a drought to prove that He was the Lord of the earth. While the Israelites chased after Baal, who was no god at all, Yahweh used famine and fire to prove His power and presence. Through the prophet Elijah, God called His people to stop wavering and choose whom they would serve. God used extreme measures to show His people that He loved them and wanted them to live in a relationship with Him.

The spirit of Elijah's message was that God loved His people and wanted them to repent and turn back to Him. Today we will find a deeper insight into Elijah's message in the very last few verses of the Old Testament.

Read Malachi 4:5-6 in the margin, and answer the following questions:

What prophet did God say He was sending before the day of the Lord arrives?

5"Look, I am sending you the prophet Elijah before the great and dreadful day of the LORD arrives. 6His preaching will turn the hearts of fathers to their children, and the hearts of children to their fathers. Otherwise I will come and strike the land with a curse."

(Malachi 4:5-6)

What would this prophet's preaching accomplish?

Malachi's prophecy echoed the message Elijah had preached throughout his lifetime: respond to the God who loves you or experience the consequences of separation from God. We have the benefit of the full revelation of God. In the Gospel of Luke we get a glimpse into the identity of the second coming of Elijah that Malachi prophesied. It began with Zechariah and Elizabeth, a couple who would have a child in their old age. Elizabeth was the cousin of Mary, the mother of Jesus. Her husband, Zechariah, was a priest who encountered an angel while he was ministering in the temple.

Read Luke 1:13-17 in the margin on the following page and answer these questions:

What did the angel instruct Zechariah to name his son?

Extra Insight

Remember that Elijah's name was his message and his mission. His name means "Yahweh is my God." He longed for people to know Yahweh instead of wasting time and energy on counterfeits.

What were some of the phrases used to describe John?

What specific references from Malachi 4:5-6 are found in these verses?

When Malachi said that Elijah would come in the future, he was referring to the message of Elijah through John the Baptist. We find this confirmed in several other passages in Matthew:

> "And from the time John the Baptist began preaching until now, the Kingdom of Heaven has been forcefully advancing, and violent people are attacking it. For before John came, all the prophets and the law of Moses looked forward to this present time. And if you are willing to accept what I say, he is Elijah, the one the prophets said would come. Anyone with ears to hear should listen and understand!"
>
> (Matthew 11:12-15)

> Then his disciples asked him, "Why do the teachers of religious law insist that Elijah must return before the Messiah comes?" Jesus replied, "Elijah is indeed coming first to get everything ready. But I tell you, Elijah has already come, but he wasn't recognized, and they chose to abuse him. And in the same way they will also make the Son of Man suffer." Then the disciples realized he was talking about John the Baptist.
>
> (Matthew 17:10-13)

These passages confirm that John the Baptist fulfilled the prophecy that Elijah would come and "turn the hearts of the fathers to their children, and the hearts of children to their fathers" by pointing them to repentance and to the One coming after him—Jesus Christ.

In your own words, how would you explain what it means to "turn the hearts of the fathers back to their children and the hearts of the children to their fathers"?

How does a close relationship with God through Christ affect your family relationships?

God's love and sacrifice for each of us causes us to recognize our own fallibility. Embracing God's Father-heart of love for us in the midst of our own struggle with sin helps us heal from insecurities and gives us compassion for

13But the angel said, "Don't be afraid, Zechariah! God has heard your prayer. Your wife, Elizabeth, will give you a son, and you are to name him John. 14You will have great joy and gladness, and many will rejoice at his birth, 15for he will be great in the eyes of the LORD. He must never touch wine or other alcoholic drinks. He will be filled with the Holy Spirit, even before his birth. 16And he will turn many Israelites to the LORD their God. 17He will be a man with the spirit and power of Elijah. He will prepare the people for the coming of the LORD. He will turn the hearts of the fathers to their children, and he will cause those who are rebellious to accept the wisdom of the godly."

(Luke 1:13-17)

Extra Insight

While John the Baptist claimed not to be Elijah returning (John 1:20-23), he wasn't fully aware of his own role in the divine calendar. However, Jesus confirmed that Elijah had returned through the ministry of John the Baptist (Matthew 11:13-14).

others. This takes some of the pressure off our human relationships because we are no longer expecting them to be the primary source of our love and security.

Through Elijah, Yahweh radically expressed His love toward His people; but they did not respond by turning back to Him. Later the spirit of Elijah's message was expressed through the ministry of John the Baptist, who was sent to prepare the way for Jesus as he called the people to turn back to God. In Luke 3:3 we read, "Then John went from place to place on both sides of the Jordan River, preaching that people should be baptized to show that they had repented of their sins and turned to God to be forgiven."

John and Elijah had many other similarities as well:

- Both confronted evil rulers. (1 Kings 18:17-18; Matthew 14:3-4)
- Both are described as having a rough appearance. (2 Kings 1:8; Matthew 3:4)
- Both spent time in the wilderness. (1 Kings 17:3; Matthew 3:1)
- Both called people to repent and turn to God. (1 Kings 18:21; Luke 3:3)
- Both dealt with an evil queen. (1 Kings 19:2; Matthew 14:6-8)

John the Baptist came in the spirit of Elijah to prepare people for the coming of the Messiah. His desire was for fathers' hearts to be turned toward their children, and for children's hearts to be turned toward their fathers. While Malachi 4:6 uses the word *fathers* specifically, the greater interpretation is the general concept of reconciling all people toward one another. The New International Version translates the Hebrew word *ab*, which means "father,"[2] as "parents." The consistent message is that God wants to reconcile people to Himself and to one another. His desire is that we would turn toward one another rather than neglect or fight against one another.

God is the ultimate Father. He knows that you will not find spiritual stamina apart from a close relationship with Him. As we see His Father-heart more clearly, we learn to depend on Him for strength through every season of life.

Now, I want to acknowledge that you may not have had a very good earthly example of a father-heart. Perhaps your father abandoned, neglected, or abused you. That can make it challenging to embrace God as a good Father.

No matter what kind of relationship you have had or haven't had with your earthly father, what are some general things a good father would do for his children?

I thought of things such as love, provide, protect, and discipline. Throughout Scripture we find that God's character is that of a loving Father who wants the very best for His children.

Read the following verses and underline some of the fatherly qualities of God:

Father to the fatherless, defender of widows—
> *this is God, whose dwelling is holy.*
>> **(Psalm 68:5)**

*The L*ord* is like a father to his children,*
> *tender and compassionate to those who fear him.*
>> **(Psalm 103:13)**

*My child, don't reject the L*ord*'s discipline,*
> *and don't be upset when he corrects you.*
*For the L*ord* corrects those he loves,*
> *just as a father corrects a child in whom he delights.*
>> **(Proverbs 3:11-12)**

So if you sinful people know how to give good gifts to your children, how much more will your heavenly Father give good gifts to those who ask him.
>> **(Matthew 7:11)**

All praise to God, the Father of our Lord Jesus Christ. God is our merciful Father and the source of all comfort.
>> **(2 Corinthians 1:3)**

See how very much our Father loves us, for he calls us his children, and that is what we are!
>> **(1 John 3:1b)**

Put a star beside the verse that speaks most personally to you right now.

As we understand God's Father-heart toward us, we see the message of Elijah more clearly. Elijah was a man of faith and prayer. He made choices to follow Yahweh rather than counterfeits. Through difficult seasons requiring soul care, he learned to rely on God. Even though he didn't always understand, he surrendered to God's way. Alongside his mentee Elisha and groups of prophets, he worked out his faith in the context of relationships. He left a legacy that ultimately was fulfilled as John the Baptist prepared the way for the Messiah.

God the Father has a love for us that will never fail.

God used Elijah to call the people of Israel to turn their hearts back toward Him, their loving Father. In the same way, He calls us to turn from our sin and lean into a close relationship with Him, our heavenly Father who loves us. All our earthly fathers have imperfections, but God the Father has a love for us that will never fail. He is a protector and provider who shows great compassion toward us. He also will discipline us like a good Father when we stray off the path. Yet even then He is merciful and gracious, calling us away from things He knows are not good for our souls.

I hope that you sensed God's Father-heart of love for you personally through our study today and will continue to grow deeper in His love in the weeks and months ahead.

Talk with God

Take some time to think about God's Father-heart toward you. Ask the Lord to give you eyes to see Him clearly so that you can trust Him more fully.

DAY 3: MISTAKEN IDENTITY

Today's Scripture Focus

Matthew 16:13-17;
Mark 8:27-30;
Luke 9:18-20

As we've learned some concepts of spiritual stamina from the prophet Elijah, we've had to wade through some pretty radical circumstances that are foreign to our modern experience—a prophet publicly declaring a drought is coming, worshipers of foreign gods dancing and cutting themselves in a contest on a mountain, God sending down fire to ignite an offering. Elijah's methods and ministry are not the normal fare for the average follower of Christ. However, if we can rise beyond the differing cultural climate and extreme measures used toward a rebellious people, we can catch some glimpses of our own Messiah.

Yesterday we discovered that John the Baptist fulfilled the promise of Elijah's return set out in Malachi's prophecy at the end of the Old Testament. Today we will find that, as with many other great figures of the Old Testament, we can identify some parallels between Elijah and Christ. Many scholars have explored this topic, including one who wrote these words:

> The many references to Elijah in the Gospel narrative reflect a deep expectation and an awareness that in Jesus, as in Elijah, someone larger than life is on the scene. Thus the hope of Elijah becomes an interpretive device for identifying and glorifying Jesus, the embodiment of Yahweh's full power become visible and active.[3]

By looking at the connections between Elijah and Jesus, we remember again the power and hope we have in Christ and are able to worship Him actively and fervently. This is my hope as we look into some New Testament references to the prophet we've been examining over these past weeks of our study.

We must remember that because of Malachi's prophecy that Elijah would return, the Israelites were expecting him to come and rescue them. Yet after Malachi's prophetic words were penned, four hundred years of silence ensued. This was the intertestamental period between the time of the prophets and the birth of Christ. During this period there were a number of significant changes—the number of Israelites increased greatly and they were living together in one land, and they came under Roman rule under the jurisdiction of an Edomite king.[4] God's final words to His people had been a reminder to keep His laws and a promise to send Elijah to turn the hearts of the fathers and their children toward one another (Malachi 4:4-6). After this God was silent, which means that no other prophets rose up with messages from God. While some speculate that this pause built momentum for the coming of the Messiah, we can't really know the mind of the Father about this.

What we do know is that by the time Jesus came on the scene, the Israelite people were desperate for help from Yahweh. Roman oppression and taxes had left them impoverished and controlled. Many devout followers still would have been hanging onto God's promise of rescue through Elijah. We saw this as people speculated about John the Baptist being Elijah, but we will find today that others thought Jesus fulfilled the promised return of Elijah.

In three of the four Synoptic Gospels, we find a conversation between Jesus and his disciples about this very topic.

Select one of the following passages, and read the account of Jesus discussing his identity with his disciples. Then answer the following questions.

Matthew 16:13-17
Mark 8:27-30
Luke 9:18-20

What question did Jesus ask his disciples?

What were some of the ideas that people had about Jesus' identity?

When Jesus asked what the disciples thought about who He truly was, which disciple answered? What did he say?

In these Gospel passages, John the Baptist, Elijah, Jeremiah, and some other prophets are mentioned as possibilities for the identity of Jesus. However, Peter got it right. Jesus was not Elijah. He was and is the Messiah, the Son of the living God.

Now that you have studied Elijah's life and ministry, why would you guess some people might have thought that Jesus was Elijah?

Perhaps Malachi's prophecy led people to see Christ as Elijah—or it may have been the many parallels between their stories.

Do any of the experiences, miracles, and/or messages of Elijah and Christ seem similar to you? Look over the following chart, underlining any similarities or connections that particularly stand out to you.

	Elijah	Jesus
Preparation	Elijah spent time in the wilderness cut off from society at the Kerith Brook, where he was fed by ravens. This was a season of preparation for future ministry (1 Kings 17:2-6).	Jesus spent forty days fasting in the wilderness before He began His earthly ministry (Matthew 4:1-2).
Message	Elijah's message was reflected in his name, "Yahweh is God." He preached against idolatry, specifically Baal worship. He rebuked King Ahab and leaders of Israel for leading people away from true worship of Yahweh. He called people to repent and follow God (1 Kings 18:21).	Jesus preached that people should turn from sin and turn to God (Matthew 4:17). He also specifically called out the religious leaders for their hypocrisy, referring to them as blind guides (Matthew 23:13-36). Jesus also lifted up the Father, saying He lived in total dependence on the Father and taught His message (John 5:19-23).

Miracles	Elijah showed that Yahweh was Lord over the weather when he called for a famine (1 Kings 17:1). God used Elijah to multiply the oil and flour in the containers of the widow of Zarephath (1 Kings 17:14). Elijah raised the dead son of the widow back to life (1 Kings 17:19-23).	Jesus exercised God's power over the weather when He calmed a storm (Mark 4:35-41). Jesus multiplied the fish and loaves to feed a multitude of people (John 6:1-15). Jesus raised the son of a widow back to life (Luke 7:11-17).
Promise	When Elisha asked for a double portion of the Spirit, Elijah said if he saw him going up to heaven he would receive it (2 Kings 2:9-10).	Jesus said his followers would do greater works than he had done (John 14:12).
Departure	Elijah didn't die but went up to heaven in a whirlwind alongside chariots of fire while his mentee Elisha watched (2 Kings 2:11).	After Jesus died on the cross, He came back and appeared to His disciples. Later He was taken up to heaven while His disciples watched Him (Acts 1:9-11).

Elijah was an incredible prophet. It is no wonder that when Jesus came, people confused Him with Elijah (Luke 9:7-8). When Jesus was on the cross, some people thought he was calling out to Elijah to come and help him: "Some of the bystanders misunderstood and thought he was calling for the prophet Elijah. One of them ran and filled a sponge with sour wine, holding it up to him on a reed stick so he could drink. But the rest said, 'Wait! Let's see whether Elijah comes to save him'" (Matthew 27:47-49). Elijah was a great prophet who never died but was taken up to heaven. However, Jesus is so much more! He is the Messiah, our Savior. Elijah was a man of God; Jesus *is* God.

This is a very important distinction. We can learn much from the life of Elijah. He persevered in serving God through every season of his life. He had seasons when he experienced confusion and God's power, exhaustion and renewal, confrontation and rest, listening and acting in faith, teaching and learning in community. He learned to rely on God and boldly believe Him through the highs and lows of life and ministry. We can learn from his stamina and be inspired by his faith.

One of the greatest legacies of Elijah is that he points us to Christ. As we see in the chart, he provides us with a few glimpses of the Messiah. This is his greatest legacy. The only way to heal our broken relationship with God and turn the hearts of fathers and children back toward each other is through Christ. His gospel message brings us the stamina we need to continue following God even when we want to quit. Each of us must answer the question Jesus posed to His disciples: "Who do you say that I am?"

One of the greatest legacies of Elijah is that he points us to Christ.

If someone asked you to describe who Jesus is to you, what would you say?

Jesus can be many things to us depending on the circumstances we are encountering. At times He is a friend, counselor, protector, provider, or even a disciplinarian if we have gone off course. But for each of us who claims to follow Him, He always is our Savior. Let's end our time today reviewing the simple gospel message that Jesus has truly saved us from the penalty and power of sin—and one day will save us from the very presence of sin.

Read each verse, and below it write a simple gospel concept that summarizes its message. I have done the first one for you.

"For this is how God loved the world: He gave his one and only Son, so that everyone who believes in him will not perish but have eternal life."

(John 3:16)

Summary: <u>God loves us.</u>

For everyone has sinned; we all fall short of God's glorious standard.

(Romans 3:23)

Summary:_____

But God showed his great love for us by sending Christ to die for us while we were still sinners.

(Romans 5:8)

Summary:_____

But to all who believed him and accepted him, he gave the right to become children of God.

(John 1:12)

Summary:_____

After reviewing these verses, how do these gospel truths resonate with you personally?

These verses reveal to us what sets Christ apart from John the Baptist, Jeremiah, Elijah, or any other prophet. Only Christ could save us from our sin and reconcile us to God.

Whether these are new concepts for us or truths we've known and experienced from childhood, they can renew our faith each time we read them as they remind us of God's love and sacrifice on our behalf. It is not about what we've done or left undone; salvation comes down to faith. Ephesians 2:8-10 says it so well:

> God saved you by his grace when you believed. And you can't take credit for this; it is a gift from God. Salvation is not a reward for the good things we have done, so none of us can boast about it. For we are God's masterpiece. He has created us anew in Christ Jesus, so we can do the good things he planned for us long ago.

God wants us to do good things; He planned for us to do them long ago. However, the order is so important. He doesn't love us and save us because we do good things. Our faith in Christ *results* in salvation so that none of us can boast. Out of our love and relationship with God, who initiated a relationship with us and loves us dearly, we then desire to serve Him with a whole heart. As we near the end of our study of Elijah, I pray that his legacy of pointing us to Christ is a great source of stamina for you!

Talk with God

Thank God today for the gift of Christ. Ask God to give you the stamina you need through the power of Christ to keep walking in faith in your particular circumstances, whether through trials or blessings.

DAY 4: TAKING THE LONG VIEW

Several years ago my husband, Sean, and I took our four children out West to see some amazing places such as the Grand Canyon, Yellowstone National Park, and Mount Rushmore. For parts of the trip, we traveled with family and friends, who flew out to Denver to meet us. We thought it would be much more fun, however, to drive cross-country in our minivan, putting six thousand miles on old "Miss Scarlet"—as we called her—in three weeks. Many times Sean and I heard comments like "Are we there yet?" and "She's touching me!" and "Can I charge my phone now?"

The van time wasn't the highlight of the trip, to say the least. The best antidote for the long hours of travel came when we discussed the destinations.

Today's Scripture Focus

Matthew 17:1-13

I had a travel book and periodically asked the kids to unplug from their devices so that I could describe the next stop. We would talk about where we would eat, places we would hike, and the history of some of the national parks and monuments. In order to endure the grueling aspects of the trip, we needed to focus on where we were headed.

Similarly, when we hit challenging seasons in life, we can gain spiritual stamina as we focus on our final destination. Through Christ, God has promised us eternal life. I can't wrap my mind around the concept of eternity. I live by a calendar full of starting and ending times and dates. Yet God tells us that beyond this life is another one that goes on forever. Elijah reminds us of this as he appears in the New Testament hundreds of years after he ascended in a whirlwind into the sky. His life didn't end when his earthly ministry was over.

Thinking about heaven and eternal life can motivate us to persevere through the trials of this life.

Read Matthew 17:1-13 and answer the "who" questions below:

Who did Jesus take up on the mountain? (v. 1)

Who suddenly appeared and was talking with Jesus? (v. 3)

Who had the bright idea to make shelters as memorials? (v. 4)

Who spoke from a voice in the cloud? (v. 5)

Who was terrified and fell down on the ground? (v. 6)

I'm sure Peter, James, and John must have been bursting at the seams to tell others that they had seen Moses and Elijah. Imagine hearing about great leaders of God's people who lived hundreds of years before your lifetime and then getting to encounter them personally. I can only imagine what it would be like to meet some of the missionaries or great leaders of the past such as John Wesley, C. S. Lewis, or Helen Keller.

What Bible character or Christian leader from the past is someone you would be excited to meet?

When I read this passage, I wonder how the disciples recognized Moses and Elijah. They didn't have photographs or the Internet back then. Did the Lord just reveal their identities to them? We do not read that the disciples actually spoke to Moses or Elijah, though we know that Jesus was talking with them. These verses remind us of the eternal nature of our souls.

We can get so caught up with the problems and issues of today. Sometimes we are in crisis mode as we're facing relationship problems, health challenges, or grief. Other times we just feel down for no apparent reason. The other day I texted a good friend to see how she was doing, and this was her response, "I'm fine. Feel meh but have no good reason. I'm like a modern day Grinch right now. I don't know what my deal is—I'm just in a blah mood all the time."

I've had days or weeks when I could have been the author of that text. I bet you have as well. When we get in that kind of funk, we need perseverance. Those are the days to remember that this life is not all there is. We are on a journey, and we haven't arrived at our ultimate destination. Scripture actually instructs us to think about eternity.

> **We are on a journey, and we haven't arrived at our ultimate destination.**

Read the following verses and write a key word or phrase below each one to summarize its message:

Since you have been raised to new life with Christ, set your sights on the realities of heaven, where Christ sits in the place of honor at God's right hand. Think about the things of heaven, not the things of earth.
(Colossians 3:1-2)

Key Word or Phrase: _____

"Seek the Kingdom of God above all else, and live righteously, and he will give you everything you need."
(Matthew 6:33)

Key Word or Phrase: _____

And we are instructed to turn from godless living and sinful pleasures. We should live in this evil world with wisdom, righteousness, and devotion to God, while we look forward with hope to that wonderful day when the glory of our great God and Savior, Jesus Christ, will be revealed.

(Titus 2:12-13)

Key Word or Phrase: _____

These are just three of many passages that remind us to think about, seek, and look forward to heaven. By taking the long view of life, we can lean into God's strength through all the different seasons of life. Elijah lived for a kingdom far beyond the nation of Israel. God spoke messages through him reminding his people not to live for the moment but, instead, to follow His Word.

Taking the long view of life usually means not doing what feels good in the moment in order to do what ultimately will satisfy. This is true when it comes to our money. Dave Ramsey is an author and radio talk show host who often repeats the phrase, "Live like no one else now so you can live and give like no one else later."[5] He teaches that by living within your financial means by disciplining yourself today, you will avoid the costs associated with debt and penalties as well as the pitfalls that often accompany overspending.

The same is true when it comes to our physical health. I want to live on chocolate chip cookies and hot chocolate. They taste so good! But if I learn to take the long view when it comes to my body, I know that I will not feel my best if these types of foods become my steady diet. I have to discipline myself to exercise and eat healthy foods, occasionally having my cookies and hot cocoa in moderation.

The long view is of greatest importance when it comes to our spiritual lives. Our finances and earthly bodies are only for this life, but our souls will live on forever. So we must discipline ourselves to practice spiritual rhythms that bring life and peace to our souls. We won't get there with a steady diet that consists of watching Netflix and playing games on our phones. These things aren't wrong in their proper place; but when we are constantly seeking to be entertained rather than pursuing a relationship with God, we deprive our souls. We can learn from Elijah to think eternally.

When I attended prayer meetings as a teenager, I often heard Dr. K. P. Yohannan pray the prayer of Jonathan Edwards: "Lord, stamp eternity on my eyes."[6] These words have stuck with me since my teen years. When I get caught up thinking about my imperfect house, imperfect body, and imperfect family, wanting to throw in the towel, I can choose to pray, "God, stamp eternity on my eyes. Help me to see this from Your point of view." This is something each of us can ask God to do in our lives.

By taking the long view, we will be more motivated to pray, study God's Word, and make wise choices with our time, money, and words. With our sights set on heaven, we will realize the temporal nature of most of our problems and be able to focus on people and God's Word—the only two things that will last forever.

Who are some people or activities that help you take the long view when it comes to your spiritual life?

My mentor, godly friends, church services, daily Bible readings, and prayer journal are some of the things that help redirect me when I'm feeling blah or overwhelmed.

Just a few weeks ago, I woke up in the middle of the night worried about several different things. I tried to pray but kept reverting to worry. After almost an hour of battling, I finally got up, went upstairs, and opened my laptop. I figured that if I wasn't going to sleep, I might as well do something productive like go through my email. I hoped that might distract me and make me sleepy. I noticed an email from my friend Barb Roose, who had sent me a preview of her new *Joshua* Bible study, which is about worry. As I began to read her manuscript, God used His Word and the encouragement of my friend to remind me of the long view. My spirit stopped fretting after reading, meditating on what I had read, and asking God for help. After only twenty minutes or so, I knew I could head back to bed.

Since that night I have been free from worrying about those particular issues. In order to build stamina to give us strength in our weak moments, we must identify and rely on the people and practices that help us take the long view.

While the transfiguration account we read today was penned by Matthew, Peter actually wrote about the experience himself in one of the letters he wrote near the end of his life.

Read 2 Peter 1:16-21. What words or phrases do you find here related to the transfiguration account in Matthew?

> By taking the long view of life, we can lean into God's strength through all the different seasons of life.

What did Peter say that the transfiguration should bring in our lives? (v. 19)

What do we learn from these verses about the prophets, including Elijah, and their prophecies? (vv. 19-21)

Peter tells us that we can have great confidence in the message of prophets. We are to pay close attention to what they wrote, because their words come from God and are like a light in the darkness. My prayer for you throughout our study of Elijah has been that you are able to pay close attention to God's message for you. Perhaps He has been speaking to you about prayer, choices, soul care, surrender, mentoring relationships, or legacy as we have examined each of these facets of Elijah's ministry and message.

When I interviewed several women in their later years of life, asking them what spiritual legacy they hope to leave, they said that they wanted others to remember that . . .

- I was connected in a deep relationship with God;
- I lived love;
- I lifted up those around me;
- Jesus was my life, and I want everyone else to be with Him too;
- I was a friend of God; and
- I was kind.

Take some time now to focus on the long view of your life, and describe below the spiritual legacy you hope to leave for future generations. (Focus on your character and spiritual habits more than events or accomplishments.)

We remember Elijah as a man of prayer, a prophet who spoke God's messages, a human being who had questions and even felt like quitting, and a mentor who grew bolder later in life. He certainly wasn't perfect. In fact, James 5:17 tells us he was just as human as we are. Yet he left a legacy that has continued to inspire followers of God long after his earthly life.

As we think about heaven and take the long view of our circumstances, we too can endure the challenging seasons of life with hope for better days ahead!

Talk with God

Spend your prayer time today thinking about heaven. Ask God to stamp eternity in your eyes so that you can seek His kingdom as your first priority.

DAY 5: MERCY

As we come to our final day of study, we will explore one more New Testament mention of the prophet Elijah. Throughout our study, we've seen the concepts that lead to spiritual stamina fleshed out in Elijah's life:

- PRAYER
- CHOICES
- SOUL CARE
- SURRENDER
- MENTORING
- LEAVING A LEGACY

As we pursue these attributes and practices in our lives, we must be on guard against simply working a plan. Our spiritual stamina comes from a relationship with the living God. He longs to show us mercy and kindness as we walk closely with Him. While we can grow in endurance through spiritual rhythms and relationships, our ultimate weapon against weariness is found in knowing and loving God. We all encounter seasons when we feel alone. Many times we have more questions than answers. God longs to help us understand His ways but also calls us to trust Him when we can't.

Read Romans 11:1-6 and describe the season of Elijah's ministry to which this passage refers:

Today's Scripture Focus

Romans 11:1-6, 13-24, 33-36

Our ultimate weapon against weariness is found in knowing and loving God.

When Elijah felt alone, Yahweh told him that seven thousand others had not bowed their knees to Baal. He reminded Elijah that the plan was bigger than his individual pursuit of God.

When you have been discouraged either by the response of others or by challenging circumstances, how has the Lord reminded you of His presence and plan?

When we grow weary, God often sends people or experiences to remind us of His truth. Just as Yahweh encouraged Elijah in a still small voice, He encourages us today through His word, His people, and the nudges of His Holy Spirit. In Elijah's life we see God's love and kindness on display.

Look again at Romans 11:5-6, and answer the questions below:

How many remained faithful, and how was this possible? (v. 5)

What do we learn about God's grace in verse 6?

God's grace is free and undeserved. Though many rejected God in the days of Elijah as well as when God sent His own Son to earth, through God's grace there always has been a remnant, a small group of people who persist in following God.

Have you ever thought that the whole world was going its own way and no one seemed to be truly following God? Elijah thought that at one point, and God told him that other followers of Yahweh were out there. He was not alone. God in His kindness longs for all people to turn toward Him. Even when many rejected the Messiah, God pursued others with the gospel message.

Read Romans 11:13-24 and either draw a picture or write a description of the tree, roots, and branches that the Apostle Paul used to illustrate God's relationship with the people of Israel and the Gentiles:

Extra Insight

"Grafting describes any of a number of techniques in which a section of a stem with leaf buds is inserted into the stock of a tree." It requires tools such as a knife, hammer, saw, pruning shears, and chisel; and it can bring an injured tree back to a healthy state.[7]

We see in the illustration of a tree with both roots and branches the relationship of God with people. He is both kind and firm. He has a place for anyone who will turn to Him and follow His ways. He grafted in the Gentiles when they believed in His Son, and "if the people of Israel turn from their unbelief, they will be grafted in again, for God has the power to graft them back into the tree" (v. 23). A few verses later we find these words: "For God's gifts and his call can never be withdrawn" (v. 29). God longs to show mercy to each one of us—and that means you and me!

What God asks is that we trust Him. This isn't always easy because His ways often do not make sense to us. We have some questions we wouldn't mind asking God, such as

- Why is there so much suffering in the world?
- Why do bad things happen to good people?
- What is the best way for us to live out Your mission in our generation?

What questions would you add to these if you had an opportunity to ask God for answers face-to-face?

God doesn't answer all our questions. He leaves us with some measure of mystery and calls us to trust Him and accept His ways. The Apostle Paul ends Romans 11 concluding that we must admit that we can't make sense of some things:

[33]*Oh, how great are God's riches and wisdom and knowledge! How impossible it is for us to understand his decisions and his ways!*

34For who can know the LORD's thoughts?
    Who knows enough to give him advice?
35And who has given him so much
    that he needs to pay it back?

36For everything comes from him and exists by his power and is intended for his glory. All glory to him forever! Amen.

(Romans 11:33-36)

As we review the truths of spiritual stamina from each week of our study, let's remember that we do not know everything. We must study, question, exercise self-discipline, and pursue God wholeheartedly. And ultimately, we acknowledge that there is a point where our understanding must yield to a God who is wiser. It is impossible for us to understand all His decisions and ways. This is why we must work to build stamina through every changing season of life while also learning to accept the things we cannot change.

Instead of a Weekly Wrap-up, let's end our study by reviewing what we have learned throughout our weeks together, asking the Lord to bring to mind any additional areas of focus where we can grow in spiritual stamina in our daily lives.

Read through the following summary chart, and then draw a star beside the week that resonates most strongly with you during this season of your life.

Week of Study	Main Themes	Reflection Questions
1. Prayer (1 Kings 17)	Elijah called for a drought and then spent over a year at the Kerith Brook being fed by ravens. He had to trust God to provide for him each day. When the brook dried up, God led him to a foreign, pagan land where a widow fed him. This was a season when Elijah was cut off from his people and totally dependent on God during a time of famine. When we encounter dry seasons in life, we can grow in faith by trusting God each day. These are times when our prayer lives grow and desperation causes us to deepen our dependence on God. Elijah came to believe that Yahweh had no limits and even prayed for the widow's dead son to come back to life. We too can trust God when we turn to Him during seasons of lack and isolation.	What circumstances have caused you to feel isolated or dependent on others lately? How is the Lord calling you to grow in faith during this season of your life? What are some blessings or provision you can thank God for during a season that has seemed desperate at times? Are there any steps of obedience that the Lord is calling you to take right now, even if they don't make sense to you?

Week of Study	Main Themes	Reflection Questions
2. Choices (1 Kings 18:1-40)	Elijah chose to pray and believe God. When he issued a challenge to the people of Israel, he told them they would have to choose between serving Yahweh or counterfeits like Baal. He asked them how long they would waver between two opinions. He also declared a contest on Mount Carmel where the people could ask their gods to show themselves, and he would ask Yahweh to show Himself. Fire came down from heaven to prove who the real God of power was. However, the people had to make the choice to follow Him. In the same way, we must choose each day. Will we live for ourselves or surrender our time, thoughts, and lives to God? We all make mistakes, but the pattern of our choices will greatly affect our spiritual stamina over the changing seasons of life.	What choices are you facing currently? How would you like to grow in your prayer life? Are there any practices that are out of balance in your life and need to be scaled back or strengthened? What spiritual practices would you like to focus on in the coming weeks to grow in self-control?
3. Soul Care (1 Kings 18:41–19:18)	Some seasons of life cause us to grow weary and feel like giving up. Sometimes we can identify the causes of our soul fatigue, and other times we have no idea why each step seems so difficult. After God showed Himself in a great display of fire on Mount Carmel, Elijah found himself running for his life again. He told God he had had enough. The Lord didn't scold him but instead sent an angel to minister to him with food and rest. During some seasons of life, we need to eat, rest, and heal. After Elijah was strengthened, the Lord sent Him on a journey and spoke to him in a still small voice. He challenged Elijah to go back the way he had come, find other God followers, and fulfill his original calling as a prophet. As we listen to God in seasons of soul care, He can reignite our passion to follow Him.	What has been contributing to your weariness lately? What are some ways you can slow down and care for your soul? Are there some things you need to take a break from in order to make prayer and rest a priority? What adjustments is the Lord calling you to make so He can prepare you for future service?

Week of Study	Main Themes	Reflection Questions
4. Surrender (1 Kings 19:19–22:9)	As Elisha accepted the prophetic call from Elijah, he had to say no to farming and family in order to say yes to God. We too must surrender to God's call on our lives. We must discern where God is calling us to say yes and what He is asking us to leave behind. We also must learn to accept many things that don't make sense to us. Naboth experienced injustice that angered the Lord. We need wisdom to know when to humbly accept things we don't understand and when to stand up against injustice.	Where is the Lord calling you to say no to some things in order to say yes to Him? How can you humbly accept God's way in any areas that clash with your logic and emotions? Is there a tangible way you can stand up for others who can't stand up for themselves? What current situation is the Lord calling you to stop fighting against and accept right now?
5. Mentoring (2 Kings 1–2)	Elijah recognized the importance of the people God placed alongside him. He mentored Elisha and had relationships with different groups of prophets in many cities in Israel. He boldly stood up to King Ahab and his son. Mentoring relationships and church community are vital to our spiritual stamina as well. We are called to make disciples and pass on God's message of love and hope to future generations. When Elijah was taken up to heaven in a whirlwind, Elisha was given a double portion of the spirit to carry on the work of proclaiming the true and living God.	Who is your mentor in the faith? Who are you mentoring? What relationships inspire you to run your spiritual race with endurance? Is the Lord calling you to be more involved in reaching out to others through your small group, Bible study group, or area of service or ministry at church?

Week of Study	Main Themes	Reflection Questions
6. Legacy (Elijah in the Old and New Testaments)	Elijah's ministry transcends the pages of 1 and 2 Kings. The prophet Malachi prophesied that Elijah would come back and turn the hearts of fathers and children back toward each other. John the Baptist came to fulfill that prophecy as a voice crying in the wilderness for people to turn from sin and turn to God. Many Israelites thought Jesus could be Elijah returning as Malachi prophesied. Elijah did end up returning to earth when Jesus was transfigured, reminding us that we must take the long view of our lives. This earthly life isn't all that exists. Elijah lives eternally just as we will. The promise of heaven gives us the stamina we need to persevere when life wears us down.	What kind of legacy do you hope to leave when your earthly days are over? How does Elijah's connection with Christ's gospel message encourage you? What lessons in spiritual stamina have you learned from Elijah's life and ministry?

How do the themes of the week that you starred echo into your current circumstances?

Now write a few brief responses to the reflection questions listed for that week (right column of the chart):

The Lord's heart for His people has not changed. God longs to help us endure in every season. Whether we are going through a dry season filled with fatigue, confusion, or relationship issues, or we are experiencing a season of celebration or rest, we can grow in spiritual stamina through a close walk with God. No counterfeits will do. Only by trusting in the Lord with the fervor and determination of Elijah will we be able to keep on going and growing, even when we feel like giving up.

The Lord loves us and longs to shower His kindness and grace upon us. This gift is free and undeserved. God calls us to trust Him and accept His ways

God longs to help us endure in every season.

even when we struggle to reconcile His methods with what we know to be true about God. While we may not go up to heaven in a whirlwind accompanied by chariots of fire as Elijah did, we can persevere to the end of our lives with a growing faith and the spiritual stamina that comes from a close walk with God. Then we will leave a legacy for future generations pointing to God's faithfulness in the journey of faith.

Talk with God

Thank God for all that you've learned about Him through Elijah's life. Ask the Lord to give you stamina to endure whatever season of life you are currently experiencing or facing.

VIDEO VIEWER GUIDE: WEEK 6

As we grasp God's Father-heart toward us, we find _____ and
_____ in our relationships.

*Malachi 4:5-6—Elijah will turn the hearts of fathers to their children and the hearts of children
to their fathers*

Luke 1:17 – The birth of John the Baptist foretold

Christ must _____ and we must _____ if we are to live out
our callings in faith.

John 3:30—"He must become greater and greater, and I must become less and less."

Taking the _____ _____ in decision-making will help us
leave the legacy we desire.

2 Peter 1:3-11—God has given us everything we need for a godly life

Hebrews 12:1-3—God's discipline proves His love

VIDEO VIEWER GUIDE ANSWERS

**Introductory Session
(Optional)**

Patriarchs

United

Divided

Israel / Judah

Prophets

Ahab

Jezebel

God

saves

human

Week 1

contact point

waiting

provides

persist

Week 2

through

counterfeits

think

Praying

Week 3

broken / overwhelmed

food / rest

still small / listen

unique work

Week 4

intimacy

mercy

theology / reality

grace

Week 5

counterfeits

caught / taught

showing up

influence / impact

Week 6

healing / purpose

increase / decrease

long view

Notes

Introduction

1. Paul R. House, *1, 2 Kings, The New American Commentary* (Nashville: Broadman and Holman Publishers, 1995), 209.

Week 1

1. A. W. Pink, *The Life of Elijah* (Carlisle, PA: The Banner of Truth Trust, 1963), 11.
2. English Oxford Living Dictionaries, s.v. "stamina," https://en.oxforddictionaries.com/definition/us/stamina, accessed January 24, 2018.
3. Angela Lee Duckworth, TED Talk, Grit: *The Power of Passion and Perseverance*, https://www.ted.com/talks/angela_lee_duckworth_grit_the_power_of_passion_and_perseverance, accessed January 18, 2018.
4. Pink, *The Life of Elijah*, 11.
5. House, *1, 2 Kings*, 205.
6. Ibid., 207.
7. Pink, *The Life of Elijah*, 13.
8. House, *1, 2 Kings*, 213.
9. Donald J. Wiseman, *1&2 Kings: An Introduction and Commentary* (Leicester, England and Downers Grove, IL: InterVarsity Press, 1993), 164.
10. Genesis 2:4, *Scofield Reference Bible Commentary*, biblestudytools.com, https://www.biblestudytools.com/commentaries/scofield-reference-notes/genesis/genesis-2.html, accessed January 24, 2018.
11. House, *1, 2 Kings*, 212.
12. Merrill F. Unger, *The New Unger's Bible Dictionary* (Chicago: Moody Bible Institute, 1988), 1193–1194.
13. Leon J. Wood, *The Prophets of Israel* (Grand Rapids, MI: Baker Book House, 1979), 209.
14. Ibid., 210.
15. Ibid.
16. House, *1, 2 Kings*, 213.
17. Wiseman, *1&2 Kings*, 164.
18. Pink, *The Life of Elijah*, 14.
19. Warren W. Wiersbe, Be *Responsible (1 Kings): Being Good Stewards of God's Gifts* (Colorado Springs, CO: David C. Cook, 2002), 158.
20. Wood, *The Prophets of Israel* , 211.
21. See House, *1, 2 Kings*, 210; Unger, *The New Unger's Bible Dictionary*, 132, 202; and Wood, *The Prophets of Israel*, 209.

22. Walter Brueggemann, *Smyth and Helwys Bible Commentary: 1 & 2 Kings* (Macon, GA: Smyth and Helwys Publishing, 2000), 209.

23. Frank E. Gaebelein, *The Expositor's Bible Commentary* (Grand Rapids, MI: Zondervan, 1988), 4:138.

24. Wiseman, *1&2 Kings*, 165.

25. Wood, *The Prophets of Israel*, 222.

26. Wiseman, *1&2 Kings*, 165.

27. Wood, *The Prophets of Israel*, 212.

28. Brueggemann, *Smyth and Helwys Bible Commentary: 1 & 2 Kings*, 210.

29. Watchman Nee, *The Normal Christian Church Life* (Anaheim, CA: Living Stream Ministry, 1980), 161.

30. Gaebelein, *The Expositor's Bible Commentary*, 138.

31. Wiseman, *1&2 Kings*, 166.

32. Phillip Yancey, *Prayer: Does It Make a Difference?* (Grand Rapids, MI: Zondervan, 2006), 219.

Week 2

1. Walter Brueggemann, *Smyth and Helwys Bible Commentary: 1 & 2 Kings* (Macon, GA: Smyth and Helwys Publishing, 2000), 221.

2. Frank E. Gaebelein, *The Expositor's Bible Commentary* (Grand Rapids, MI: Zondervan, 1988), 4:141.

3. Brueggemann, *Smyth and Helwys Bible Commentary*, 221.

4. Ibid.

5. Gaebelein, *The Expositor's Bible Commentary*, 4:142.

6. Donald J. Wiseman, *1&2 Kings: An Introduction and Commentary* (Leicester, England and Downers Grove, IL: Inter-Varsity Press, 1993), 167.

7. Gaebelein, *The Expositor's Bible Commentary*, 4:142.

8. Dale Ralph Davis, *1 Kings: The Wisdom and The Folly*, Focus on the Bible Commentary Series (Ross-shire, Scotland: Christian Focus Publications, 2002), 229.

9. Ibid., 231.

10. Wiseman, *1&2 Kings*, 168.

11. Jim Dethmer, Diana Chapman, and Kaley Warner Klemp, *The 15 Commitments of Conscious Leadership: A New Paradigm for Sustainable Success* (Dethmer: Chapman and Klemp, 2014), 15.

12. Wiseman, *1&2 Kings*, 168.

13. Choon-Leong Seow, *The New Interpreter's Bible Commentary* (Nashville: Abingdon Press, 2015), 2:712.

14. Wiseman, *1&2 Kings*, 168.

15. Brueggemann, *Smyth and Helwys Bible Commentary*, 224.

16. Gaebelein, *The Expositor's Bible Commentary*, 4:146.

17. Davis, *1 Kings*, 232.

18. Ibid., 233.

19. Paul R. House, *The New American Commentary, 1, 2 Kings* (Nashville: Broadman and Holman Publishers, 1995), 204.

20. Leon J. Wood, *The Prophets of Israel* (Grand Rapids, MI: Baker Book House, 1979), 212.

21. Davis, 1 *Kings* 234.

22. Wiseman, 1&2 *Kings*, 169.

23. House, *1, 2 Kings*, 220.

24. Gaebelein, *The Expositor's Bible Commentary*, 4:146.

25. Ibid., 4:147.

26. Iain W. Provan, *Understanding the Bible Commentary Series: 1 & 2 Kings* (Grand Rapids, MI: Baker Books, 1995), 138.

27. Davis, 1 *Kings*, 240.

28. Ibid., 242.

29. House, *1, 2 Kings*, 220.

Week 3

1. Mark Batterson, *The Circle Maker: Praying Circles Around Your Biggest Dreams and Greatest Fears* (Grand Rapids, MI: Zondervan, 2011), 33–34.

2. Walter Wink, *Engaging the Powers: Discernment and Resistance in a World of Domination* (Minneapolis: Fortress Press, 1992), 322.

3. Dale Ralph Davis, *1 Kings: The Wisdom and The Folly*, Focus on the Bible Commentary series (Ross-shire, Scotland: Christian Focus Publications, 2002), 248.

4. Leon J. Wood, *The Prophets of Israel* (Grand Rapids, MI: Baker Book House, 1979), 214.

5. Donald J. Wiseman, *1 & 2 Kings: An Introduction and Commentary* (Leicester, England and Downers Grove, IL: Inter-Varsity Press, 1993), 171.

6. Ibid., 172.

7. Davis, *1 Kings*, 267.

8. Wiseman, *1 & 2 Kings*, 171.

9. Frank E. Gaebelein, *The Expositor's Bible Commentary* (Grand Rapids, MI: Zondervan, 1988), 4:148.

10. Ibid.

11. Paul R. House, *The New American Commentary, 1, 2 Kings* (Nashville: Broadman and Holman Publishers, 1995),222.

12. Iain W. Provan, *Understanding the Bible Commentary Series: 1 & 2 Kings* (Grand Rapids, MI: Baker Books, 1995), 144.

13. Davis, *1 Kings*, 266.

14. Provan, *Understanding the Bible Commentary Series*, 144.

15. Wiseman, *1 & 2 Kings*, 172.

16. Ibid.

17. Frank E. Gaebelein, *The Expositor's Bible Commentary* (Grand Rapids, MI: Zondervan, 1988), 149.

18. Ibid., 150.

19. *Baker's Evangelical Dictionary of Biblical Theology*, s.v. "theophany," http://www.biblestudytools.com/dictionaries/bakers-evangelical-dictionary/theophany.html, accessed January 24, 2018.

20. Walter Brueggemann, *Smyth and Helwys Bible Commentary: 1 & 2 Kings* (Macon, GA: Smyth and Helwys Publishing, 2000), 236.
21. Davis, *1 Kings*, 263.
22. Gaebelein, *The Expositor's Bible Commentary*, 150.

Week 4

1. Donald J. Wiseman, *1 & 2 Kings: An Introduction and Commentary* (Leicester, England and Downers Grove, IL: Inter-Varsity Press, 1993), 174.
2. Leon J. Wood, *The Prophets of Israel* (Grand Rapids, MI: Baker Book House, 1979), 217.
3. Dale Ralph Davis, *1 Kings: The Wisdom and The Folly*, Focus on the Bible Commentary Series (Ross-shire, Scotland: Christian Focus Publications, 2002), 274–275.
4. Jonathan Minnema quoting J.I. Packer, "18 J. I. Packer Quotes that will Change Your Faith," *Converge Magazine*, https://www.convergemagazine.com/18-j-i -packer-quotes-that-will-challenge-your-faith-17358/, published January 18, 2016, accessed February 1, 2018.
5. Walter Brueggemann, *Smyth and Helwys Bible Commentary: 1 & 2 Kings* (Macon, GA: Smyth and Helwys Publishing, 2000), 246.
6. Davis, *1 Kings*, 292–293.
7. Ibid., 305.
8. Wiseman, *1 & 2 Kings*, 184.
9. C. S. Lewis, *Mere Christianity* (New York: HarperCollins, 1952), 305.
10. Davis, *1 Kings*, 303–308.
11. John Stott, "Pride, Humility & God," Sovereign Grace Online, September/ October 2000, http://www.sovereigngraceministries.org/sgo/v18no5/prt _pride.html, accessed August 3, 2005.
12. Serenity Prayer, commonly attributed to Reinhold Niebuhr, http://www. thevoiceforlove.com/serenity-prayer.html; http://www.nytimes.com/2008/07/11 /us/11prayer.html?_r=o, accessed February 1, 2018.
13. Wiseman, *1 & 2 Kings*, 186.
14. Iain W. Provan, *Understanding the Bible Commentary Series: 1 & 2 Kings* (Grand Rapids, MI: Baker Books, 1995), 169.
15. Davis, *1 Kings*, 315.
16. Paul R. House, *The New American Commentary, 1, 2 Kings* (Nashville: Broadman and Holman Publishers, 1995), 253.

Week 5

1. Paul R. House, *The New American Commentary, 1, 2 Kings* (Nashville: Broadman and Holman Publishers, 1995), 243.
2. Iain W. Provan, *Understanding the Bible Commentary Series: 1 & 2 Kings* (Grand Rapids, MI: Baker Books, 1995), 169.
3. House, *1, 2 Kings*, 253.
4. Donald J. Wiseman, *1 & 2 Kings: An Introduction and Commentary* (Leicester, England and Downers Grove, IL: Inter-Varsity Press, 1993), 192.

5. Ibid., 193.
6. House, *1, 2 Kings*, 253.
7. Strong's H982, s.v. "batach," https://www.blueletterbible.org/lang/lexicon /lexicon.cfm?t=kjv&strongs=h982.
8. Wiseman, *1 & 2 Kings*, 193–194.
9. Walter Brueggemann, *Smyth and Helwys Bible Commentary: 1 & 2 Kings* (Macon, GA: Smyth and Helwys Publishing, 2000), 289.
10. Ibid., 294.
11. House, *1, 2 Kings*, 210.
12. W. J. Weatherby, *Chariots of Fire* (New York: Quicksilver Books, Inc./Dell Publishing Co. 1981), 87.
13. Provan, *Understanding the Bible Commentary Series*, 173.
14. Timothy Keller, *Prayer: Experiencing Awe and Intimacy with God* (New York: Penguin Random House, 2014) 20.
15. Brueggemann, *Smyth and Helwys Bible Commentary*, 297.
16. Wiseman, *1 & 2 Kings*, 196–197.
17. Strong's 06484, s.v. "patsar," https://www.biblestudytools.com/lexicons /hebrew/kjv/patsar.html, accessed February 8, 2018.
18. Strong's 954, s.v. "buwsh," https://www.bibletools.org/index.cfm/fuseaction /Lexicon.show/ID/H954/buwsh.htm, accessed February 8, 2018.

Week 6

1. Jewish Virtual Library, s.v. "Elijah," http://www.jewishvirtuallibrary.org/elijah, accessed February 13, 2018.
2. The KJV Old Testament Hebrew Lexicon, Strong's 01, s.v. "ab," https://www .biblestudytools.com/lexicons/hebrew/kjv/ahttp://www.thetransformedsoul .com/additional-studies/spiritual-life-studies/the-intertestamental-period -and-its-significance-upon-christianityb.html, accessed February 13, 2018.
3. Walter Brueggemann, *Smyth and Helwys Bible Commentary: 1 & 2 Kings* (Macon, GA: Smyth and Helwys Publishing, 2000), 290.
4. D. W. Ekstrand, "The Intertestamental Period and Its Significance upon Christianity," http://www.thetransformedsoul.com/additional-studies /spiritual-life-studies/the-intertestamental-period-and-its-significance -upon-christianity, accessed February 15, 2018.
5. Dave Ramsey, "Tired of Keeping Up With the Joneses," https://www. daveramsey.com/blog/tired-of-keeping-up-with-the-joneses, accessed February 15, 2018.
6. K. P. Yohannan, "Twenty-Fifth Anniversary," https://www.gfa.org/kpyohannan /5-minutes-with-kpyohannan/twenty-fifth-anniversary/, accessed February 16, 2018.
7. Leonard B. Hertz, "Grafting and Budding Fruit Trees," Yard and Garden, University of Minnesota Extension, https://www.extension.umn.edu/garden /yard-garden/fruit/grafting-and-budding-fruit-trees/, accessed February 16, 2018.

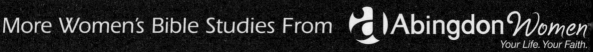
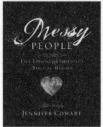

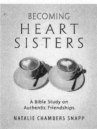

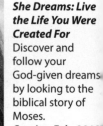

More from *Melissa Spoelstra*

Bible Studies

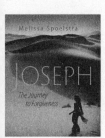

Numbers: Learning Contentment in a Culture of More

Workbook ISBN: 9781501801747

Say no to the desire for bigger, better, faster, and more.

First Corinthians: Living Love When We Disagree

Workbook ISBN: 9781501801686

Show love when you disagree without compromising your convictions.

Joseph: The Journey to Forgiveness

Workbook ISBN: 9781426789106

Find freedom through forgiveness.

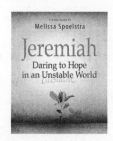

Jeremiah: Daring to Hope in an Unstable World

Workbook ISBN: 9781426788871

Learn to surrender to God's will and rest your hope in Him alone.

Books

Total Family Makeover: 8 Practical Steps to Making Disciples at Home

ISBN: 9781501820656

Discover a practical approach to helping your children learn what it means to be followers of Christ.

Total Christmas Makeover: 31 Devotions to Celebrate with Purpose

ISBN: 9781501848704

Help your family learn what it means to truly celebrate their Savior.

Abingdon *Women*
Your Life. Your Faith.